From Bitcoin to Bored Apes:

The Rise and Fall of the Crypto Dream

Copyright © 2024 Crypto Critic.
All rights reserved. This book or any portion thereof may not be reproduced or used in any manner whatsoever without the express written permission of the publisher except for the use of brief quotations in a book review.

Introduction: The NFT Phenomenon..3
Chapter 2: The Economic Collapse of 2008............................ 4
Chapter 3: The rise of Bitcoin... 13
Chapter 4: The Revolution of Ethereum...............................27
Chapter 5: Proof of Work and Proof of Stake........................ 37
Chapter 6: Crypto's Challenges as Currency........................ 48
Chapter 7: Non-Fungible Tokens Explained.........................56
Chapter 8: The Mechanics of NFTs..60
Chapter 9: The NFT Gold Rush...63
Chapter 10: The NFT Hype and Its Critics............................ 68
Chapter 11: The $69 Million Beeple Sale...............................73
Chapter 12: Exploring the NFT Community.........................76
Chapter 13: Fraud and Deception in the NFT Market........ 83
Chapter 14: Toxic Positivity and the NFT Echo Chamber 101
Chapter 15: The Limitations of NFT Functionality........... 105
Chapter 16: The Role of Wallet Managers............................108
Chapter 17: Privacy Concerns in the Blockchain................ 116
Chapter 18: NFTs as Access Passes...126
Chapter 19: The Squid Game Token Scam...........................129
Chapter 20: Play-to-Earn Games and the Axie Infinity Case. 134
Chapter 21: The Dystopian Reality of the Play-to-Earn Model..145
Chapter 22: Deflation and Its Impact................................... 152
Chapter 23: The DAO Illusion...165
Chapter 24: The Limitations of DAOs.................................. 168
Chapter 25: The Corporatization of Everything.................184
Conclusion: Deteriorating System...186

Introduction: The NFT Phenomenon

For digital content creators, the unavoidable topic of 2021 has been NFTs.

From embarrassingly awkward ape avatars to shockingly distasteful tributes to departed celebrities, and even six-figure transactions for the "original version" of a meme, it is the phenomenon currently dominating the collective mindset of digital artists and monopolizing all the attention in the room.

And I genuinely want to discuss this; I want to share my views on NFTs, digital ownership, and scarcity, exploring all the various facets of the issue. However, I can't solely focus on NFTs because, in the end, they serve as a representation of something much broader, and it is that "something more" that ultimately holds significance.

Chapter 2: The Economic Collapse of 2008

So, allow me to share a story.

In 2008, the economy effectively collapsed.

The fundamental chain reaction was as follows:

Banks introduced a concept known as mortgage-backed securities, a financial instrument that could be traded or accumulated based on a collection of thousands of individual mortgages. Due to banks' general hesitance to issue mortgages, stemming from their risk aversion in lending vast sums of money that would be paid off over decades, these bonds were perceived as especially stable. However, they were also immensely lucrative for the banks issuing both the mortgages and the bonds.

Because of this perceived stability, many financial institutions, such as pension funds and hedge funds, incorporated them as the foundation of their investment portfolios.

In this scenario, a mortgage becomes more profitable for the bank that issues it as part of a bond than it does as an isolated mortgage. Proportionately, the returns per mortgage from the bond are significantly better than those from the individual mortgage.

There are some issues, though. The first problem is that the highest returns on a bond occur when it first enters the market; a new bond that generates new securities sales is valued more highly than an older bond that is gradually appreciating but not experiencing much trading. The second problem is that there is a limited number of people and houses in America; the market must stabilize at a natural ceiling since eventually, nearly all mortgages are encapsulated into bonds, leaving very few new bonds that can be created and sold.

Thus, the following incentives are established. One: it benefits banks when there are more houses for which they can issue mortgages. Two: the greater the number of mortgages issued, the better, because a problematic mortgage is worth more as part of a bond than a good mortgage that isn't bundled into a bond.

Consequently, real estate developers find it quite easy to secure funding from banks to create sprawling new suburbs filled with houses that can be sold to generate mortgages. However, instead of constructing the types of housing that most people genuinely need and want, they focus specifically on the upper-middle-class homes that align with the preferences of banks packaging the bonds. Buyers, in turn, find it almost suspiciously easy to obtain a mortgage, despite the fact that, for most individuals, the economy wasn't thriving. Wages were stagnant, and even though developers were wildly constructing new housing, the properties being built were all beyond their financial reach, and paradoxically, this significant increase in supply wasn't driving down prices.

This occurred because the houses were being purchased, just not primarily by individuals intending to reside in them.

They were being acquired by speculators who would then either rent them out or often leave them vacant with the intention of selling them a couple of years later.

As speculators were purchasing the available supply, it generated artificial demand. Prices continued to rise as speculators kept buying, creating the illusion that value was increasing, which attracted more speculators who bought up additional supply and further inflated prices.

These speculators were enabled by a system prioritizing the generation of new mortgages solely for the sake of increasing the number of mortgages to be bundled into bonds.

Down payments were low, and mortgages came with enticing teaser rates, meaning that during the first three to seven years of the mortgage, the monthly payments were minimal, sometimes as low as a few hundred dollars per month for a mortgage that would typically charge thousands.

Caught up in all this were genuine buyers who had been lured into signing for a mortgage they could not afford by aggressive salespeople motivated to generate mortgages that they could then sell to a bank that would package them into a bond for pension funds, all because it's beneficial when the line goes up.

It was a bubble.

The bubble burst as the teaser rates on the mortgages began to expire, causing monthly costs to skyrocket, and since the demand was artificial, there were no actual buyers for the speculators to sell the houses to.

As a result, the speculators began unloading their holdings, which ultimately drove prices down, but due to the original inflated prices, the new prices remained unattainable for most actual buyers.

Legitimate buyers caught in the middle experienced a spike in their rates, but as the prices of the houses decreased due to speculators attempting to liquidate their holdings, the price of the house fell relative to the mortgage issued, preventing them from refinancing and trapping them into paying the original terms.

Unable to sell their homes and afford the monthly payments, both legitimate owners and speculators defaulted on their mortgages and ceased payments.

Eventually, the default rate reached a critical level, leading to the failure of the bonds.

As the bonds collapsed, it impacted all first-order buyers of the bonds, such as hedge funds, pension funds, retirement savings funds, and so forth.

It also cascaded through all derivatives, which are financial products that derive their value directly from the value of the bond.

This resulted in a knock-on effect: vast segments of the economy turned out to be dead weight, rotten to the core. Yet as a decayed tree falls, it still damages its neighbors and crushes anything beneath it.

This was a failure brought about by a mixture of greed, active fraud, and willful ignorance at every level of authority.

The banks issuing the faulty mortgages were the same banks selling the bonds and supplying the capital to construct the houses that would generate the mortgages.

The ratings agencies assessing the bonds were publicly traded entities reliant on maintaining good relations with the banks, incentivized to rubber-stamp whatever rating would please their clients. The regulatory bodies that should have anticipated the issues were depleted by budget cuts and caught in conflicts of interest as employees utilized their regulatory positions to secure higher-paying jobs in industry.

And, to top it all off, the individuals primarily responsible for the chaos were well aware that as they and their toxic products were so deeply intertwined with the economy's foundations, they could rely on a government bailout because, no matter how corrupted they were, they were still quite large entities.

This blatant display of greed and fraud created fertile ground for both anti-capitalist and hyper-capitalist movements: both groups perceiving themselves as being wronged by the system, with one faction diagnosing the issue as the system's inherently corrupt and corrupting incentives, while the other viewed the crisis as a result of excessive regulation and exclusion.

The hyper-capitalist or anarcho-capitalist stance argues that in a less constrained market, there would be greater incentive to call out wrongdoing, that regulation merely succeeded in creating an in-group capable of conspiring without competition.

Of course, this argument fails to acknowledge that a significant number of individuals within the system did, indeed, amass considerable wealth specifically by betting against the synthetic success of the market, but I digress.

Chapter 3: The rise of Bitcoin

Into this environment in 2009, Bitcoin emerged, an entirely electronic peer-to-peer currency.

Philosophically, Bitcoin and cryptocurrency in general were heralded as a means to eliminate banks and centralized currency.

This would serve as the foundation, both philosophically and technologically, on which NFTs would be built. It's quite a journey from here to the Bored Ape Yacht Club, so prepare yourself. Buckle up.

As we delve into this, we'll need to navigate a lot of terminology and complexity.

Some of this complexity arises from systems that are technically intricate, while some stems from poorly designed or intentionally convoluted systems meant to obfuscate understanding and thus lend an air of legitimacy.

The entire topic resides at the intersection of two fields notoriously prone to hype-fueled confusion: computer technology and finance, inheriting a plethora of bad habits from both, with a reputation for making things intentionally more complicated to create the illusion that only they possess the intelligence to comprehend it.

Mining and minting are both methods for creating tokens, the fundamental elements that blockchains interact with, but colloquially, they refer to different processes.

Mining is a coin token generated as a product of the consensus protocol, while minting is a user-initiated addition of a token to a blockchain.

All blockchains are composed of nodes, which can be watcher nodes, miner nodes, or validator nodes, although most miner nodes also act as validator nodes. Fractionalization is the process of taking one asset and creating a new asset that represents portions of the original.

So you end up with $DOG, a memecoin crypto DeFi venture capital fund backed by the fractionalization of the original Doge meme sold as an NFT to PleasrDAO on the Ethereum network.

I apologize; some of this is just going to be like that.

The concept behind cryptocurrency is that your digital wallet functions similarly to a bank account, eliminating the need for a bank to hold and process your transactions.

Instead of containing a sum that conceptually represents physical currency, the cryptocoins in your wallet are the actual money. And because this money isn't issued by a government, it is resistant to historical cash crises like hyperinflation caused by governments intentionally or unintentionally devaluing their currency. It brings the flexibility and anonymity of cash and barter into the digital realm, enabling individuals to transact without oversight or intermediaries.

In a concise pitch, you can see the allure; there's a compelling narrative there.

However, in the twelve years since then, none of this has unfolded as envisioned.

Bitcoin was inherently too slow and costly for regular commerce.

From the outset, it effectively emerged as a speculative financial vehicle, and thus the only consumer market that proved viable was buying and selling illegal drugs, where the high fees, rapid price fluctuations, and multi-hour transaction times were mitigated by receiving LSD in the mail a week later.

Regarding banking, Bitcoin was never designed to address the actual issues created by the banking industry; it was merely intended to be the new medium through which they operated. The principal offering wasn't revolution but, at best, a changing of the guard. The grievance isn't with the outcomes of 2008, but rather with the necessity of being well-connected to participate in the grift back in 2006.

Even the change of the guard is an illusion.

Old money finance figures like the Winklevoss twins were among the first notable names to dive into crypto, where they remain today.

Financial criminal Jordan Belfort, convicted of fraud for orchestrating pump-and-dump schemes and permanently barred from trading regulated securities or acting as a broker, is a cryptocurrency enthusiast.

Venture capitalist Chris Dixon, who profited immensely from the "old web" in his role as a general partner at VC firm Andreessen Horowitz Capital Management, is a prominent figure in the NFT realm. He likes to portray himself as an outsider fighting against gatekeepers, yet he also sits on the boards of Coinbase, a major cryptocurrency exchange profiting by serving as the gatekeeper and collecting fees on all entries and exits to the crypto economy, and Oculus VR, owned by Meta, formerly Facebook.

Peter Thiel, who transitioned from wealthy to ultra-wealthy during the Web2 boom via PayPal, is a crypto advocate and associates with several eugenics supporters who promote cryptocurrency as a return to "sound money" for a plethora of extremely racist reasons, as when they reference banks and bankers, they are alluding to Jews.

Some of the largest institutional holders of cryptocurrency are precisely the same investment banks that contributed to the subprime mortgage crash.

Rather than serving as a reprieve for those harmed by the housing bubble—individuals whose savings and retirements were, unbeknownst to them, being gambled away—cryptocurrency quickly became the new playground for opportunists.

It's crucial to emphasize this point: cryptocurrency does nothing to resolve 99% of the banking industry's issues, as those problems are rooted in human behavior.

They're incentives, social structures, modalities. The issue concerns what people are doing to others, not the building where the actions take place bearing the word "bank" on the façade.

In addition to failing to address problems, Bitcoin also came with a significant drawback.

Bitcoin's innovation over previous attempts at digital currency was the implementation of a distributed append-only ledger, a type of database where new entries can only be added to the end, and various nodes, known as validators, compete to determine who gets to validate the next update.

These components are the blockchain and proof-of-work verification.

Now, proof-of-work has an intriguing history as a technology, typically deployed as a deterrent against misconduct. For instance, requiring that every email sent necessitates the user's computer to solve a simple math problem imposes a trivial burden on normal users sending a few dozen or even a couple of hundred emails daily, while placing a massive load on anyone attempting to spam millions of emails.

In Bitcoin, the process works as follows: when a block of transactions is ready to be recorded on the ledger, all mining nodes in the network compete to solve a cryptographic math problem based on the data within the block.

Essentially, they compete to discover the equation that yields a specific result when the contents of the block are inputted, with the complexity of the desired result deliberately increasing based on the total processing power available to the network.

Once the math problem is solved, the rest of the validation network can easily verify the work, as the contents of the block can be fed into the proposed solution, which either produces the correct answer or fails.

If the equation is correct and the consensus of validators approves it, the block is appended to the ledger, and the miner who solved the problem first is rewarded with newly generated Bitcoin.

The complexity of the answer the computers are attempting to solve scales with the network's processing power, specifically to create substantial diminishing returns as a safeguard against an attack on the network where someone simply builds a more powerful computer and takes control.

Critics have pointed out that this gives rise to new issues: adversarial validation will deliberately incur escalating processing costs, generating perverse structural incentives that rapidly reward capital holders while locking out individuals who are not already exceedingly wealthy. Although the increasing proof-of-work scheme incurs heavy diminishing returns, returns are still returns, meaning more will always go to those with resources to construct larger rigs.

Regardless of the envisioned future of Bitcoin, at present, computer hardware can be purchased with dollars.

Instead of dismantling corrupt power structures, this merely became a new tool for existing wealth.

And that's… precisely what occurred.

Thus commenced an arms race for ever-larger processing rigs, followed by rising demands for support systems, hardware engineers, HVAC, and operating space necessary to house those rigs.

And don't worry, we won't overlook the power requirements.

These rigs consume an industrial amount of power, and due to the winner-takes-all nature of the competition, enormous amounts of redundant work are being performed and discarded.

Estimating this power consumption is challenging; the data is very complex, dispersed across hundreds of operators globally, who frequently move in search of cheap electricity, and is heavily politicized.

However, even conservative estimates from within the crypto-mining industry suggest that the total energy cost of Bitcoin processing is comparable to that of a small industrialized nation.

Now, advocates will retort that the global banking industry also consumes a significant amount of power, citing things like idle ATMs humming through the night, which is technically not untrue. In factual terms, the entire global banking industry does, in fact, utilize a considerable amount of electricity.

But to provide context, it takes six hours of that sustained power draw for the Bitcoin network to process as many transactions as VISA handles in one minute, and during that time, VISA uses mere fractions of a cent of electricity per transaction.

And that's just VISA. That's one major institution.

So, yes, globally, the entire banking industry consumes a lot of power, and a non-negligible portion of that is waste that could be better allocated.

However, it's also the global banking industry serving seven billion people, rather than the niche interest of a few hundred thousand gambling enthusiasts.

To address all this upfront, Bitcoin and proof-of-work cryptocurrency are not incentivizing a shift toward green energy sources like solar and wind; rather, they are offsetting it.

Because electrical consumption, electrical waste, is the value that underpins Bitcoin.

Miners expend X dollars in electricity to mine a Bitcoin, and they anticipate being able to sell that coin for at least X plus profit.

When new power sources are introduced and the price of electricity decreases, they do not lower X; they construct a larger machine.

Chapter 4: The Revolution of Ethereum

In 2012, Vitalik Buterin, a crypto enthusiast and disgruntled Warlock main, set out to rectify what he perceived as Bitcoin's shortcomings and inflexibilities.

Rather than becoming the new digital currency—something people actually used for purchases—Bitcoin had transformed into an unwieldy speculative financial instrument, too slow and costly for anything beyond extravagant purchases of luxury cars.

It was plagued by money laundering and burdened with negative press.

After the FBI shut down Silk Road, you couldn't even use it to buy drugs anymore.

In practice, you couldn't do anything with your Bitcoin except speculate, locking up funds in hopes that Bitcoin would rise later, while praying you wouldn't lose it all to a scam, lose access to your wallet, or have it stolen by an exchange.

The result, launched in 2014, was Ethereum, a competing cryptocurrency that boasted lower fees, quicker transaction times, a reduced energy footprint, and, most notably, sophisticated processing functionality.

While the Bitcoin blockchain merely tracks the location and movement of Bitcoins, Ethereum would be more expansive. In addition to tracking Ether coins, the ledger could also monitor arbitrary blocks of data.

As long as they were compatible with the structure of the Ethereum network, those blocks of data could even be programs utilizing the validation network as a distributed virtual machine.

Vitalik envisioned this as an expansive, infinite machine, duplicated and distributed across thousands or millions of computers—a system where the entire history of a new internet could be immutably recorded, immune to censorship, and impossible for governments to dismantle.

He foresaw it dismantling banks and other intermediary industries, allowing everyone to be their own bank, their own stockbroker, bypassing governments, regulators, and insurance agencies.

His peers imagined a future where Ethereum became not just a repository for financial transactions, but also for identity, with deeds, driver's licenses, professional credentials, medical records, educational achievements, and employment history transformed into tokens and stored immutably and eternally on the chain.

Through crypto and the Ethereum virtual machine, they believed they could offer all the advantages of Wall Street investors and Silicon Valley venture capitalists to the world's poorest individuals—the unbanked and forgotten.

This lofty philosophy is elaborated upon in detail in the journalistic piece *The Infinite Machine* by former journalist-turned-crypto-advocate Camilla Russo.

The book is genuinely intriguing, not for the quality of the writing—Russo fails to critically assess the validity or rationale behind even the simplest claims, skirting just shy of hagiography by occasionally noting that something was a tad tacky or embarrassing, but only just barely.

She recounts ornate tales about the impoverished individuals that Vitalik and his associates claimed they were working to assist, yet never once contemplates that the proposed solutions might not actually function or that the individuals claiming to want to solve those issues might not even be addressing them.

This is a significant concern, as the entire crypto space, throughout the time period covered by Russo's book, was inundated with astroturfing schemes where two individuals would visit a small community in Laos or Angola, take numerous photos of people at a "crypto investing seminar," generate headlines for their coin or fund, and then vanish.

For years, individuals were asking vendors if they could place a Bitcoin sticker on their cash registers, as the optics of making it appear that a location accepted Bitcoin was cheaper and easier than actually using Bitcoin as a currency.

We have an entire decade filled with credulous articles claiming that Venezuela and Chile are on the verge of transitioning entirely to crypto, based solely on the assertions of two trust fund individuals from San Bernardino.

A whole ten years littered with discarded press releases about Dell, Microsoft, and Square introducing crypto to consumers before quietly discontinuing their services after a year or two upon realizing the demand simply wasn't there.

The fact that the development of Ethereum heavily relied on a $100,000 fellowship grant from Peter Thiel is mentioned, but the ideological ramifications of that connection are never examined; the entire subject occupies merely a single paragraph sprinkled as flavor into a narrative about Vitalik and his co-developers airing their grievances regarding some petty infighting.

The book is primarily valuable as a point of reference against reality.

It serves as a very thorough, albeit uncritical, record of absolutely bizarre claims.

"The idea was that traits of blockchain technology—such as having no central point of failure, being uncensorable, cutting out intermediaries, and being immutable—could also benefit other applications besides money.

Financial instruments like stocks and bonds, and commodities like gold, were the obvious targets, but people were also discussing putting other representations of value like property deeds and medical records on the blockchain, too. Those efforts—admirable considering Bitcoin hadn't, and still hasn't, been widely adopted as currency—were known as Bitcoin 2.0."

I find this paragraph particularly compelling because it illustrates just how disconnected from reality the individuals actually building cryptocurrencies are.

They lack an understanding of the ecosystems they aim to disrupt; they only know that these are things that can be conceptualized as valuable and assume that because they grasp one very complicated concept—programming with cryptography—all other complex matters must be simpler and naturally lower in the hierarchy of reality, easily driven by the hammer they have forged.

The notion of placing medical records on a public, decentralized, trustless blockchain is utterly nightmarish, and anyone proposing it should be immediately discredited.

The fact that Russo fails to question any of this is a glaring example of journalistic malpractice.

In terms of advancements over Bitcoin, Ethereum boasts many. It's not particularly challenging.

Bitcoin is lacking.

However, Ethereum resolves none of Bitcoin's issues and introduces a new array of problems fueled by the technofetishistic egotism of believing that programmers are uniquely equipped to tackle societal challenges.

Vitalik wants his invention to be an infinite machine, so let's consider what that machine is designed to do.

To truly grasp the full scope of this, we need to delve deeper into the technical aspects, because that technical functionality informs the behavior of the entire system.

In a very McLuhan-esque manner, the machine shapes its surrounding environment.

As previously mentioned, a blockchain consists of two broad fundamental components: the ledger and the consensus mechanism.

All currently popular blockchains employ an append-only ledger.

Now, this is not particularly remarkable on its own.

Append-only is merely a database setting that permits new entries to be added to the end of the current database; once something is recorded in the database, it becomes read-only. Standard applications are typically things like activity logs, which is conceptually what a blockchain essentially is: a massive log of transactions.

The catch is that it's decentralized, with voluntary participants hosting a complete copy of the entire log, and this is where the second component, the consensus mechanism, comes into play.

All validating participants, referred to as nodes, possess a complete copy of the database, and no single copy is considered the authoritative version.

Instead, a consensus mechanism determines which transactions genuinely took place.

This is where proof of work comes into play.

Chapter 5: Proof of Work and Proof of Stake

Proof of work isn't the sole consensus mechanism, but it's popular because it's easy to implement by simply cloning Bitcoin and is resilient against the types of attacks that crypto enthusiasts are concerned about.

It's a very brute-force solution, but genuinely, if you want a network of ledgers where no one trusts anyone else, requiring everyone on the network to perform extreme amounts of wasted, duplicate work is one way to achieve that.

One of the key problems this machine addresses is the double-spend problem: how do you prevent someone from spending the same dollar twice?

If someone attempts to do so, how do you ascertain which transaction actually occurred?

Banks resolve this issue by not correlating account balances with any specific dollar, processing transactions on a first-come-first-served basis, which they monitor with central resources, and penalizing users with overdraft fees for double-spending.

By eschewing a central solution, cryptocurrencies depend on their consensus mechanism.

The most prevalent alternative to proof of work is proof of stake, in which validators post some form of collateral, usually the currency endemic to the chain, with the amount of collateral influencing their odds of receiving the validation reward for a given transaction. The primary proposal of proof of stake is that it significantly reduces the energy waste associated with proof of work, though it is less resilient than proof of work.

In terms of energy costs, proof of stake remains inefficient, simply due to the sheer volume of redundancy, but on a per-user basis, it is at least inefficient on the scale of a game rather than a steel mill.

This is challenging to assess, as the most popular proof of stake chains are still relatively unpopular and low-traffic in the grand scheme of things, heavily centralized.

Claims about scalability are supported solely by the creators' assertions.

Proof of stake is also considerably more complex because there must be a mechanism for determining who gets to perform the validations and how audits are conducted, along with the question of who controls that system and whether someone can seize control of it or the entire stake by simply purchasing the staking pool, and so on.

Proof of stake also, even more explicitly, rewards the wealthy who possess the capital to both stake and spend. It's also even more overtly exclusionary. Ethereum's proposed migration to proof of stake has a buy-in requirement of 32 Ether, which, at the time of writing, is approximately $130,000, meaning only early adopters and the affluent can genuinely participate meaningfully beyond just crumbs.

This, in turn, exacerbates inherent issues with the long-term growth of the chain.

Even if you resolve the escalating energy demands of proof of work, the data requirements for storing the chain and participating as a validator are also prohibitive in a way that inevitably centralizes power in the hands of a few wealthy operators.

Vitalik: 85 terabytes per year is totally manageable, right? Like, because, uh, 85 terabytes per year, if you have even one individual who just keeps purchasing, like, um, a hundred-dollar hard drive, like, uh, I think once every month, then they can store it, right? Like, it's something like that. So it's too large for just a casual user who wants to run the chain on their laptop, but one dedicated user who cares can totally afford to, uh, keep the chain stored. So 85 terabytes, not a big deal, right? But once you increase that number, it starts becoming a serious issue.

The major downside of all these systems is that they're incredibly slow. Proof of work is inefficient by design, and proof of stake is burdened with several layers of randomness that must be executed before any transaction can occur, and particularly suffers from delays when chosen validators are offline, necessitating a new draw.

As an extension of being slow, they're also susceptible to becoming overwhelmed if too many individuals attempt to make transactions simultaneously, which can result in desynchronization between validators and even lead to what's known as a fork, where two or more groups of validators reach differing conclusions about the state of the network, and each branch continues on afterwards, assuming it is the authoritative version.

Forks can also be intentionally caused, and in fact, this is the only effective way to reverse transactions. If someone were to steal your coins, the only means of recovering them would be to persuade the individuals managing the chain itself to negotiate a rollback.

That's foreshadowing for later.

Now, due to the nature of a fork involving disagreement on what transactions actually transpired and who received payment for those transactions, this means that each branch of the fork has a vested interest in its own branch being the legitimate one, so resolving forks can evolve into irreconcilable divisions. This might be amusing for an outside observer viewing it as trivial internet drama, but it is frankly unacceptable for anything claiming to be a serious and legitimate currency.

It's crucial to emphasize that because of the chain's nature, the way the ID numbers of later blocks depend on the outcomes of previous blocks, these aren't just a few disputed transactions that need resolution between the buyer, the seller, and the payment processor; these are disagreements regarding the fundamental state of the entire economy that create an entirely alternate reality.

It's an ecosystem that thoroughly dismantles consumer protections and renders their reimplementation extremely challenging.

One of the significant selling points of all this technology is that it's particularly secure, exceedingly difficult for anyone to hack directly, owing to the substantial redundancy.

A great deal of emphasis is placed on the system's resilience against man-in-the-middle attacks, which are your classic Hollywood hacker-type scenarios.

Someone sends a command from point A, and on the route to point B, it is intercepted and altered.

Someone hacks into the bank and adds an arbitrary number of zeros to their account balance.

Proponents frequently assert that blockchain could transform the global shipping industry and reduce fraud.

This claim warrants scrutiny.

First, the items that blockchain can track are things that manufacturers and shippers are already tracking, or at least attempting to track, so this is not so much "revolution" as it is "standardization."

Even that is built on the assumption that everyone adopts the same chain.

It's an extremely optimistic assumption.

Countless firms deliberately prefer their information to remain centralized and obscured to guard against corporate espionage.

The absence of a shared, standardized repository for all information is not a result of it being previously impossible; it is because it has been undesirable.

Second, it presumes the existence of a theoretical mechanism ensuring the synchronization of the chain and reality beyond the current capabilities of logistics software, some means of preventing individuals from simply falsifying information on the blockchain and providing it with the expected data — the blockchain equivalent of ripping off the shipping label and applying it to a new box.

The more significant issue is that, in the realm of fraud, man-in-the-middle attacks are relatively uncommon.

Global shipping must contend with it in certain circumstances, but overall, the vast majority of fraud does not originate from altering information during transit but rather from colluding parties entering false information from the outset.

Con artists don't hack the system to transfer your funds to offshore accounts; they persuade you to divulge your password.

Most fraud arises from individuals who technically have permission to perform their actions.

Rather than preventing these common types of fraud, cryptocurrency has made them absurdly easy, and the primary reason cryptocurrency needs to be so resistant to man-in-the-middle attacks is that the decentralized nature of the network otherwise makes it acutely vulnerable to those attacks.

What this all essentially indicates is that blockchains are generally ineffective at accomplishing most of their intended functions, and many innovations within blockchains are attempts to resolve problems that blockchains themselves introduced.

Chapter 6: Crypto's Challenges as Currency

The most significant challenge cryptocurrencies face is the lack of tangible goods to use them for as currencies, such as rent, food, or transportation, which is due to fairly straightforward reasons.

One reason is that transaction fees on popular chains are so exorbitant that it's pointless to utilize them for any transaction that isn't in the hundreds or thousands of dollars; no one is going to buy the Bitcoin Bucket from their local KFC. Ethereum's primary transaction fee, known as Gas, on a good day hovers around $20, but that's an overly optimistic estimate.

As of December 2021, the daily average cost of Gas hasn't fallen below $50 since August, with the three-month daily average exceeding $130.

And that's just the daily average.

The hourly price can, and does, fluctuate by as much as two orders of magnitude.

The throughput of blockchains is so dismal that transaction slots are auctioned off to the highest bidder; that's why these figures are so extreme.

It only takes a few high rollers competing on a transaction to drive the hourly price of Gas above $1,000. The internal term for this phenomenon is a "gas war" because it's that common.

Bots, in particular, can inflate gas prices into the tens of thousands of dollars as they compete to seize on mistakes, such as someone listing an item for sale far below its general market price.

Additionally, it's important to note: these gas wars are not confined to just the item being fought over. If Steam is overwhelmed because ConcernedApe unexpectedly released Stardew Valley 2, that will likely remain fairly contained. If Taylor Swift concert tickets go on sale and LiveNation faces a surge, you might never even hear about it.

What those situations don't do is cause the cost of placing an order on DriveThruRPG to spike by eight thousand percent for three hours.

The second major reason is that the value of the coins themselves is so volatile that unless you're willing to engage with the speculative nature of the coins, accepting them as payment for anything entails a significant risk.

Bitcoin, in particular, suffers from issues where the value of the coin can fluctuate dramatically between the initiation and completion of a transaction due to its sluggish transaction times.

This has resulted in the emergence of a whole layer of intermediaries within the ecosystem—so-called "stablecoin" exchanges like Tether that exist to facilitate rapid transfers between cryptocurrencies and lock in values.

Stablecoins, instead of having a speculative value, are pegged to the value of actual currencies, such as the Euro or US dollar.

The underlying problem they aim to solve is twofold.

Firstly, converting cryptocurrency into dollars triggers accountability to the tax authorities, and the primary goal of crypto in general is to undermine public services, so that's off the table.

Secondly, there simply aren't enough buyers, and the liquidity within the ecosystem is insufficient to cash out substantial holdings.

Tether, the largest stablecoin, used to market itself as being backed on a one-to-one basis when it was called Realcoin, but that language has grown considerably more obscure over time as it has become apparent that it simply isn't true.

This is a highly complicated situation, but the short version is that the individuals who own Tether also own a legitimate money exchange called Bitfinex, and evidence suggests that the two services, both of which require having real dollars on hand to back their products and facilitate exchanges, are sharing the same pool of funds, swapping it back and forth as necessary.

This means that at any given moment, either service could potentially be backed by zero dollars, or at least that's what the data implies might be the case.

The point is that if you're a high roller with tens of millions of conceptual dollars tied up in cryptocurrency, there's a fundamental cash issue. Your holdings have inflated to tens, hundreds, or thousands of times what you initially invested, but that price is merely theoretical. It's speculative.

You possess all this crypto, but you can't meaningfully spend it, and there aren't enough buyers for you to liquidate it.

In order for you to cash out, you must persuade someone else to buy in.

When viewed holistically, these factors mean that cryptocurrency is a Bigger Fool scam.

There's been a lot of digital ink spilled attempting to classify it as a decentralized Ponzi scheme, a pyramid scheme, or some hybrid of the two, which is a taxonomical debate that I'm not here to resolve. However, like both of those, it operates as a Bigger Fool scam.

The entire structure of cryptocurrencies, at its basic operational level, is designed to reward the earliest adopters the most, regardless of whether you're discussing proof-of-work or proof-of-stake. This is inherent to their existence.

As Stephen Diel succinctly stated, "These schemes around crypto tokens cannot create or destroy actual dollars; they can only shift them around. If you sell your crypto and make a profit in dollars, it's only because someone else bought it at a higher price than you did. And then they expect to do the same, and so on ad infinitum. Every dollar that comes out of cryptocurrency must come from a later investor putting a dollar in. Crypto investments cannot be anything but a zero-sum game, and many are actually massively negative-sum. To presume a crypto investment functions as a store of value, we simultaneously need to assume an infinite chain of greater fools who keep buying these assets at any irrational price into the future forever."

With all that established, let's address the ape in the room.

Chapter 7: Non-Fungible Tokens Explained

NFTs, or non-fungible tokens.

On a conceptual level, the technology acts as a sort of generic database to facilitate the exchange of digital assets.

The most optimistic interpretation of it is a framework for a type of computer code that creates so-called true digital objects — meaning digital objects that possess the attributes of both physical and digital items, being losslessly transmittable while offering strict uniqueness, which is a significant concept.

Strict uniqueness refers to the notion that two different items are indeed different entities, even if they are different copies of the same item.

My copy of *Grey* by EL James is strictly unique.

While millions of copies of the book exist, this is the only copy that is this particular copy, and it is the sole copy with the specific damage of being glued shut and tossed into the Bow River.

It is also strictly scarce. While millions of copies of *Grey* exist, that number is still finite, meaning it is possible, although not immediately practical, for the world to run out of copies.

NFTs impose a simulacrum of this physical scarcity and uniqueness onto digital objects within their ecosystem.

On a technical level, a non-fungible token is simply a token that has a unique serial number and cannot be divided into smaller parts.

Two tokens, even those that represent the same conceptual item, remain strictly unique with different serial numbers.

Within the context of Ethereum and its derivatives, these tokens are essentially a small data packet that can contain a payload of code.

It's a container that you can embed a micro-program into.

That micro-program is referred to as a smart contract—a term so comically self-important that I find it misleading to even call them that, but I must do so for the sake of clarity.

But just to clarify, yes, that is how the inventors envision the role of these entities—as the intersection of programming and law.

The phrase "code is law" gets tossed around as an aphorism, and it's so riddled with flaws that we'll be discussing it for an indefinite period.

Before we dive deeper into that, this is the crux of the matter: there is a significant disconnect between what NFT advocates claim they do and what they actually achieve.

However, and this is crucial, both the purported functionality and the actual functionality are both flawed.

It's all broken; none of it operates effectively, making the idea of it becoming the norm highly problematic. But the vision of what the world would resemble if all the mythologizing and over-promising were to materialize is equally disheartening.

The ultimate goal of this infinite machine is the financialization of everything.

Any potential benefits of digital uniqueness ultimately serve as a quirk—a necessary precondition for transforming everything into a stock market.

There's nothing inherently offensive about the concept of digital collectibles; frameworks and subcultures for digital collectibles have existed for decades in various contexts. However, NFTs exist to lend legitimacy and functionality to the cryptocurrencies they are built upon.

Okay, okay, okay, code is law.

Chapter 8: The Mechanics of NFTs

Now, what that little smart contract program does is determined by the token creator.

It can be a relatively sophisticated applet allowing the user to execute various commands, or it can be a simple hyperlink to a static URL of an image, or anything in between.

Most are far closer to static URLs than they are to functional programs.

This is partly because NFTs have become synonymous with digital art, but in reality, what the token represents is arbitrary.

It can be a video game item, a permission slip, a subscription, a domain name, a virus that steals all your digital assets, or a combination of all those elements.

While the concept has been around since 2015 when the framework was hastily assembled in a day during a hackathon, and the first Ethereum-implemented tokens were minted in 2017, for the general public, the narrative begins in the spring of 2021 after a series of high-priced sales of tokens minted by digital artist Beeple, culminating in a $69 million sale of a collage of Beeple's work in March via the prestigious auction house Christie's.

This high-profile sale initiated a media frenzy and an online gold rush as various minor internet celebrities rushed to capitalize on the trend, eager to be the next to cash in.

Over the course of about six weeks, the ecosystem burned through nearly every relevant meme possible.

Laina Morris, made famous on Reddit as Overly Attached Girlfriend, sold the "original screengrab" to Emirati music producer Farzin Fardin Fard for the equivalent of just over $400,000.

Zoe Roth, known as Disaster Girl, sold the original Disaster Girl photograph to Fard for the same amount.

Kyle Craven sold the original Bad Luck Brian photo for $36,000 to anonymous buyer @A.

Nyan Cat fetched nearly $600,000, with multiple variations also selling for six figures.

Allison Harvard sold Creepy Chan I and II for $67,000 and $83,000, respectively, both also to Fard.

In addition to these high-profile sales of already popular items, whale buyers like Fard were dropping four and five-figure sales on a random assortment of other artworks.

Corporations and individuals auctioned NFTs representing intangible, non-transferable concepts, like the "first tweet" or "the first text message."

Chapter 9: The NFT Gold Rush

Cryptocurrency advocates eagerly seized every opportunity to promote this new, bold, revolutionary marketplace that would liberate artists from the constraints of the gig economy and provide buyers with an immutable record of ownership of authenticated artworks stored on an eternal distributed machine.

You could be holding the next generation's Picasso! Artists could continue to earn passive revenue from secondary sales! Imagine what it will be worth in five years!

This created an atmosphere of absolute frenzy, as it seemed like anything could be the golden ticket.

Digital artists, particularly those working with mediums like generative art that are difficult to monetize through conventional avenues like physical prints, flocked to the space and, on the whole, suffered significant losses.

Critics began to question what was actually being bought and sold. Copyright? Commercial permissions? A digital file? Bragging rights?

In a vast number of cases, the answer was not very clear, and even the sellers, swept up in the promise of a payday, were not entirely certain what they had sold.

Many of the tokens merely pointed to images stored on standard servers accessible via HTTP, meaning the purchased assets were just as susceptible to link rot as anything else.

Some pointed to images stored on peer-to-peer IPFS servers, which are more resistant to link rot, as they, similar to a torrent, require only that someone keeps the file active somewhere rather than needing the original server to remain operational. However, as millions of dead torrents demonstrate, that's still a far cry from the "eternal" storage solution that advocates were claiming.

The images were stored and delivered just like any other image on the internet, easily saved or duplicated simply because, in order for your computer to display an image, it needs to download it.

Claims of digital scarcity pertain only to the token itself, not the item the token represents.

Moreover, there was no cryptographic link between the images and the tokens.

The image associated with a token could easily be altered or substituted if the person with access to the server hosting the image simply changed file names, rendering the relationship between the two tenuous and fragile in a way that undermined the assertions that this was somehow a more durable, reliable method of transacting digital art.

There was also no foundational proof of authenticity, no confirmation that the person minting the artwork was the actual creator.

This serves as a handy encapsulation of how blockchain fails to address the most prevalent issues with fraud, which tend to originate from incorrect data entering a system at the outset, not from data being altered mid-process.

Artists who voiced concerns about this system, which evidently incentivized impersonating popular artists, including deceased ones, were told it was their fault for not acting sooner; that if they had bought in and minted their work first, it would have been easy to prove the forgeries.

Because advocates don't view this as a tool or a marketplace that may or may not fit into an artist's business model, they see it as the future, thus failure to participate isn't a business decision, it's merely a mistake.

They're terrible people.

Chapter 10: The NFT Hype and Its Critics

Ultimately, the frenzy collapsed rather rapidly.

Not to belabor this point, but reposting digital art without attribution is not a new phenomenon.

Profiting off someone else's art is also nothing novel.

What's new is that NFTs represent a high-energy marketplace with an irrational pricing culture where the average buyer is easily flattered and not particularly discerning.

The potential gains are exceedingly high—much higher than a bootleg Redbubble store—the consequences are nearly nonexistent, and the market is evidently in an unsustainable state, creating an incentive to enter at the lowest possible cost before it collapses, hence the absolute epidemic of art theft.

Even the argument that artists could earn passive income from secondary sales turned out to have numerous caveats.

First, the smart contract for the token must include a function that defines royalties, so anyone who minted a token based on hype, making it sound like an inherent system function, was out of luck.

Secondly, the token lacks awareness of what constitutes a sale and cannot distinguish between a sale and a transfer, meaning it's actually the marketplace that informs the token "you're being sold" and collects the royalties.

The end result is that royalties can be easily circumvented simply by utilizing a marketplace that doesn't collect royalties or employs a different royalty collection format that is incompatible with the function the token uses.

While some sellers, both legitimate and otherwise, walked away with undeniably large payouts, hundreds of thousands of artists entered the fray only to discover that there was not a new, groundbreaking, highly trafficked audience of digital art collectors.

Instead, they encountered a closed market trading in casino chips, where the primary winners were those already connected—those who already had the means to capture the attention of the whales and the media—a market where participation necessitated investing in a cryptocurrency at a rapidly fluctuating price to cover the minting costs to showcase the work, where it would then sit, unsold.

This left those artists in a difficult position, forced to choose between absorbing the losses or trying to persuade their existing audience to invest as well.

The true beneficiaries were those with substantial cryptocurrency holdings, particularly Ethereum, which facilitated the vast majority of these high-profile purchases.

David Gerrard, author of *Attack of the 50 Foot Blockchain*, encapsulated it succinctly on his blog: "NFTs are entirely for the benefit of the crypto grifters. The only purpose the artists serve is as aspiring suckers to promote the concept of crypto—and, of course, to purchase cryptocurrency to pay for 'minting' NFTs. Sometimes the artist gets some crumbs to keep them promoting the concept of crypto."

The rush benefits them in two key ways: first, the price of Ether itself rises directly from the surge in demand; between January and May, the price of Ether escalated from $700 to $4,000, and second, there are new actual buyers who are not merely trading Bitcoin for Tether for Ether and back again, but are buying in with dollars, providing the entire system with the liquidity necessary for whales to actually cash out.

This arrangement—needing to purchase a highly volatile coin from individuals who paid far, far less for it to participate in a market they control—is why people instinctively characterize the whole setup as a scam.

If you buy in at $4,000 and compete against individuals who purchased in at $4, you're the one being duped.

It reveals the fundamental truth that these aren't marketplaces; they're casinos.

And indeed, even amidst all the rhetoric about "protecting artists," there lurked the ever-present specter of gambling: whatever you purchase now might be worth hundreds of times more later.

Frequently invoked is the contrasting proposition of a bad deal: what if you had been the person who bought in at $4?

Chapter 11: The $69 Million Beeple Sale

Let's closely examine that astonishing $69 million Beeple sale.

Independent journalist Amy Castor has done a commendable job tracking down the details in her article "Metakovan, the mystery Beeple art buyer, and his NFT/DeFi scheme," but to summarize the gist of her observations, the buyer is a crypto entrepreneur named Vignesh Sundaresan, who acquired the piece to enhance the reputation and value of his own crypto investment scheme, Metapurse, and Metapurse's own token, B.20, of which Beeple holds 2% of the total supply.

Following the Christie's sale, the reported value of B.20 surged from 36 cents per token to $23.

And that's just the anatomy of a single transaction.

The very evident conclusion observers reached was that none of this is about the art at all, but rather the speculative value; not what it's worth to you, but what it might potentially be worth to someone else in the future.

It's not a market; it's a casino, betting on the receipt for an image or video that's otherwise infinitely digitally replicable.

The item itself is immaterial as long as it can inflate a line.

This encapsulates the essence of the market and serves as a microcosm of what advocates envision as the future — the financialization of everything.

The frenzied marketplace surrounding old Reddit memes was doomed from the beginning.

There's a finite supply of meaningful originals, so to sustain the momentum, to keep the line rising, you need something additional — something less tethered to anything specific.

For roughly six years, my avatar on the Dungeons and Dragons forums was an image of a cabbage from a stock photo. So, I'm not exactly pioneering anything here.

Chapter 12: Exploring the NFT Community

Greg Isenberg sat at his computer and decided to type out, "most people who ridicule NFTs

- Own no NFTs
- Have never minted an NFT
- Have never engaged in a community
- Have never staked their NFT
- Haven't contributed to an NFT project
- Have never earned an NFT through gaming
- Missed out on BAYC, Punks, Cool Cats, etc."

This line of reasoning suggests that those skeptical of the market are just misinformed sore losers.

Occurrences like this contributed to the quite accurate view that the loudest proponents of NFTs were largely unfamiliar with internet culture overall, not particularly bright, and mostly approaching this from a financial perspective, further underscored by their Twitter bios stating "tweets are not investment advice."

In essence, these were the same individuals who created and purchased Juicero.

It also revealed that the discussions were fundamentally questionable.

How can you trust the honesty of someone touting the greatness of their $171,000 investment when your persuasion could directly benefit them by potentially increasing the value of their investment?

You need to be extraordinarily wealthy for $171,000 not to feel like a significant sunk cost, and that's undoubtedly going to affect your mindset and impact how you perceive the market.

For my part, I tweeted about several of these incidents and was, in turn, relentlessly pursued for days by irritating individuals sporting NFT profile pictures who insisted I just didn't understand and that I was missing out on the community.

So I resolved to check out the community for myself.

I began my investigation with the Cool Cats Discord, one of the communities touted as the best. I joined, sifted through days of chat logs, observed the ongoing discussions, and was ultimately unimpressed. It was, at best, unremarkable.

A key concern remained focused on the monetary worth of the tokens.

"If you invest 1 million in a cat, it's not just for Twitter, and no one would be pleased to see someone mint another one for free later. That's why punks are at 120 Eth... symbols... memes... that's where the value lies."

What stood out was the immediate flood of bot messages inviting me to other Discords.

Amid the spam I received and the Cool Cats' dedicated "shill" channel, I had an idea.

For days, I've been accepting every spam NFT Discord invite that came my way, and it's becoming overwhelming.

Stoner Cats, Oni Ronin, Magic Mushroom Club, NFTITS, The Humanoids, EtherGals, Cool Cats, Senzu Seeds, Pro Camel Riders, Long Ween Club, Stick Humans, Bumping Uglies, World of Wojak, GenMAP, DIMEZ, MagicMarblesNFT, Beverly Hills Car Club, Cash Cows, Long Neck Cartel, Pug Force, HoodPunks, Gorilla Club, Alien Archives, Betting Buddahs, Fighter Turtles Club, The Iconimals, Basement Dwellers, Wizard Man Jenkins, KATI, METAMONZ, CrazySkullz, BoxGang, Gym Punks, Unc0vered, Nitropunk, Crypto Bowls, Masquerade Massacre, Cat Colony, SkelFtees, Daffy Panda Ganging Up, Betting Kongs, Wolves of Wall Street, The Llama Farm, Happy Sharks, Teacup Pigs, Cool Llamas, Mad Carrot Gang, Barnyard Fashionistas, Sol Cities, Oink Club, Outlaw Punks, Crypto Astronuts, NFT Worlds, Panda Paradise, Time Travellers, CyberKongz, Party Ape Billionaire Club, J Corps, KwyptoKados, MetaBirds, and that's about as far as I got before pretty much giving up and finally turning off Discord DMs.

Now, this is just a tiny fraction of what's out there, yet I believe it's a fairly representative sample, and I gleaned quite a bit of insight.

For instance, the typical psychological profile of the average buyer is someone who is precariously middle class, socially isolated, and highly reactive to memes. They have minimal experience with legitimate businesses and production processes, making them unlikely to be deterred by unrealistic promises of future gains.

They feel insecure about their lack of knowledge, which renders them particularly vulnerable to flattery, especially when reassured that the sole reason for negativity is that critics simply don't comprehend.

Being precariously middle class provides them with enough disposable income to interact with a fairly expensive system, but also a potent anxiety regarding their financial future.

It goes without saying that they are preoccupied with money, and they primarily perceive technology as a means to earn.

Criticism of the system is usually met with confusion. Don't you want to profit?

Chapter 13: Fraud and Deception in the NFT Market

I also learned a lot about fraud, and how to commit it both intentionally and unintentionally.

The term "rug pull," along with its derivatives "rug" and "rugged," used to describe projects that made grand promises but then disappeared with the funds, quickly embedded itself into my vocabulary.

The market is absolutely rife with fraud and deception.

Wash trading, where you sell something to your own aliases to entice a real buyer who believes they're getting a great deal, is widespread.

Market manipulation is so prevalent and accepted that it's actually seen as bad form if project leaders don't actively engage in it, as it's deemed disrespectful to buyers if project leaders don't assist in inflating the resale price.

Also, and I really should make this clear, the art is subpar, but not in an interesting way.

It's bad in a bland, derivative manner, a low-effort garbage dump from artists who have largely abandoned the pursuit of ideas or opinions.

Derivative, lazy, unattractive, hollow, and tedious.

The capacity for original thought has long been drained from the illustrators working closely with those who refuse to stop talking about cryptocurrency, leading to an overwhelming tendency to revert to stale memes and self-congratulation.

A significant amount of cryptocurrency art ends up being art about cryptocurrency, blatantly pandering to an audience that is either profoundly uninformed or easily satisfied, and possibly both.

In the absence of any artistic insight, the void is filled to overflowing with references to doge memes, Bitcoin, Ethereum, stonks, to the moon, buy the dip, good morning, and desperate pleas for sempai Elon Musk to notice them, all delivered with the sincerity and authenticity of a Pickle Rick bong.

It's tempting to assert that my method, accepting every spam invite, was a fundamentally flawed way to dig deeper, that "obviously" accepting invites from spam bots would mostly lead me into less stable projects, but surprisingly, that wasn't the case.

I received just as much spam for successful projects like Humanoids and NFT Worlds as I did for rug-pulls like Crypto Astronuts and Hood Punks.

Overall, when examining the pitch package and the sample product, there's little material distinction between a project that's going to sell out 10,000 tokens in six hours and one that's destined to become a disaster as the project leader has a nervous breakdown and torches the mint three days post-launch after only selling 800 tokens.

Party Ape Billionaire Club sold out, raking in approximately $3.2 million, and are now flaunting their wealth by partnering with other crypto projects like the 2chains-produced NFT cartoon show The Red Ape Family, which genuinely showcases the community's deep pockets and commitment to quality.

Deep within their roadmap is the promise of commencing production on an MMORPG, a claim that buyers wholeheartedly trust.

Crypto Astronuts managed to sell 1262 of their 9485 tokens, amassing a commendable $375,000. But as appealing as that figure is, it's nowhere near sufficient to even begin executing their plan to develop a full-scale PvP-based MMO. Following the failed mint in October, the developers gradually went silent, and then, piece by piece, websites, social media accounts, and eventually the Discord itself vanished entirely.

Based on the supposed product, why should one of these projects succeed while the other fails?

The main difference, ultimately, between Party Ape Billionaire Club and Crypto Astronuts is that PABC was already flush with cash and capable of generating hype through high-priced giveaways and costly advertising.

Purchasing ad space in Times Square is particularly a specific fixation.

However, running a 10-second ad every eight minutes on one obscure billboard in Times Square isn't effective advertising, at least not externally.

All it truly accomplishes is internal propaganda, making insiders feel as though the money they've spent is buying credibility.

And if you're in a speculative bubble, wagering that someone in the future will buy you out for more than you invested, credibility is worth everything.

This is pervasive.

Even in the most established projects, those that have been around for years, there isn't really a substantive foundation; these aren't fandoms in the way you would experience them around a game, TV show, or book; the product is rather insubstantial, if not functionally nonexistent.

This is where these projects significantly differ from the artworks that fueled the speculative frenzy in the spring.

They're not presenting themselves as art worth owning for its own sake, no matter how flimsy and illusory that claim was, but as ongoing projects that you invest in.

The purchase of a token is an abstracted version of buying early stock in a company, a venture-capital-style investment in promises, which is a considerable mutation.

So, what do these phantom companies claim to do?

Almost all of them promise some form of direct financial returns.

Sometimes this comes as a vague notion that the entire venture will go "to the moon," meaning the value of the tokens will skyrocket, allowing early buyers to resell for substantial profits, or more concretely, as project leaders vow to establish, in effect, an unofficial hedge fund investing a communal pool into other crypto products.

Perhaps the most amusing of these was Betting Kongs, which aimed to create an unregulated real-money casino in which token holders would be, explicitly, part owners, and also allowed to gamble in the casino they owned.

"Betting Kongs is not your ordinary NFT project; we aim to generate passive income for our NFT owners by co-owning a casino with a profit split."

"Welcome to the whitepaper, fellow gamblers!"

"Why are we doing this? To put it simply, we love gambling and noticed how many operators out there are owned by large corporations that have no concern for the community they serve... We want to create a project where everyone playing can be a co-owner of the place they're playing and profit from it all."

If we're being honest, failure was probably the best outcome for everyone involved here.

Some promise this in the form of a more traditional media project, such as a comic book, cartoon, or movie, or all of the above.

"We have planned the creation of a series of comics dedicated to the pixel girl."

"The key image is static, or at least we believe so now. But the squeaky girl remains a seductress, so the image of breasts will be presented in various variations that our community will approve."

"Let's imagine there are 5,000 NFT holders. There's a 30 million market of comic lovers in the US... On average, every comic lover spends around 20 USD per comic per week. That means 80$ per month and 960$ per year. The total addressable market is worth 28,800,000,000 USD. Let's assume we capture 1% of this market. That's 288,000,000 USD per year based on monthly subscriptions raised in crypto. This is cash flow."

"It's nice to see some active communication, and I appreciate the effort (as announced this afternoon) to try and revive this project into something successful... The proposed path forward announced this afternoon is intriguing, and I'm prepared to support it. The only thing I'd also like to see, assuming the project can be successfully turned around, is to perhaps, in addition to some revenue sharing, have some revenue donated to Breast Cancer Research. To truly enjoy them, we should keep them happy and healthy!"

As already mentioned, many of them promise video games, often an MMO, but just as frequently, they merely promise the concept of a video game?

Okay, let me rephrase that.

They will guarantee "a video game."

That's the entirety of the promise, without clues regarding genre, style, scope, engine, or platform or how any of the tokens would relate to it. Just "a video game." If we sell 10,000 tokens for $300 each, we will begin brainstorming development ideas for a video game.

Now, all of these tend to be in collections of ten thousand, and there's an interesting quirk here.

The original model was to mint an entire collection and simply release them onto the market.

The cap comes into play solely because you need to instruct the program generating the garbage when to cease.

However, as the scheme gained traction and competition increased, it became clear that this was a fool's way of doing it since it meant paying gas fees on everything upfront, plus the gas fees on the actual sale.

So someone devised a method for minting a random output on demand, shifting the mint cost onto the buyer.

From there, it all took off like wildfire.

Very low upfront cost, extremely low risk, plus it transforms the entire system into a gacha game with differing rarity curves for attributes.

At best, these are all obfuscated gambling schemes; at worst, active scams.

And the potential for failure makes it incredibly challenging to distinguish one from the other.

World of Wojak only sold 20 tokens to 11 buyers and still pocketed over $5000.

Pro Camel Riders sold 114 tokens to 71 buyers and took home $25,000.

METAMONZ sold 722 of their 9999 tokens to 343 buyers and walked away with $211,000.

Since the average buy-in exceeds $350, the payout from failure makes success seem irrational.

What's fascinating about it all, however, is the emergent fiction of it.

These purveyors of smoke don't possess an actual product more complex than the output of a vending machine in the front of a grocery store, so they require a narrative to sell instead, resulting in a wave of vaguely defined projects pitching a token with an attached jpg representing the idea of something that could evolve into a future business.

What that business does is inconsequential, and indeed many of these projects, whether successful or not, trade in a flattering myth of decentralization where the direction of the business, down to its core product, is deferred into the uncertain future to be decided later by collective consensus.

Are we a comic book, a movie, a hedge fund, a casino, or a bimonthly curated box of snacks?

Well, that's up to the token holders to determine.

All that matters is that whatever it is, it will definitely make the value of your tokens increase, so you should absolutely buy two.

> *"One thing I learned about NFTs, if you believe something's going to be a blue chip, you should definitely purchase at least two, because you're going to get emotionally attached to one of them and you won't want to sell it, as NFTs are going to explode all over the world. If you've got a blue chip today, it's going to be incredibly more valuable in five years, or even three years, or even two years from now, than it is today."*

Regarding otherwise reputable, or at least established, brands and individuals entering the NFT space, the results tend to be incredibly lackluster and insubstantial, even by NFT standards; very low-risk, low-quality, low-engagement tokens hurriedly pushed out to capitalize on a hot buzzword, chasing the cash that's swirling around.

Tied into all this is a deeply entrenched resistance to any form of skepticism that ultimately manifests as a sort of toxic positivity.

This forms part of a complex feedback loop.

The projects, broadly speaking, lack any substantial product, existing almost entirely as promises backed by nothing more than a screenshot of a roadmap and some sample PFPs.

And, once again, I believe it's vital to keep in mind that this applies to successful projects just as much as to rug-pulls.

There really isn't any significant difference between Party Ape Billionaire Club and Betting Kongs.

Betting Kongs were never going to establish a casino, even if they hadn't crashed, and despite their Times Square billboards, PABC is never producing an MMORPG.

Both assertions are equally ludicrous, yet one of them made a substantial amount of money.

The primary product is ultimately hype, which is both insubstantial and capricious.

Negativity, both internal and external, can significantly influence people's willingness to invest in a project, and if buyers are hesitant, then you won't achieve a runaway sale, and if you don't get a runaway sale, that will likely deter buyers even more, resulting in the secondary market for tokens probably failing to form.

This is what renders enthusiasts so profoundly unreliable.

They have a significant financial stake in an intangible, volatile thing that exists entirely as a collective idea, a narrative about a potential future outcome, whose value is based entirely on public perception.

You can't trust their opinions because they're currently holding a hot potato, and as much as they claim to genuinely, really enjoy the sensation of holding a burning hot potato, do they?

Or are they merely hoping you'll catch it?

This fosters an atmosphere of toxic positivity where doubt is vigorously policed by both project leaders, who have an obvious financial interest in the hype since their big payday is during the minting rush, and community members themselves, who also have a speculative financial interest in the hype.

While all this is logical in a pure sense, as there's an effect that can be explained by an incentive, the outcome is effectively a self-organizing high-control group.

Skeptics are so harshly ostracized that it stifles all discourse regarding a project's actual viability.

All concerns are merely FUD: fear, uncertainty, and doubt.

Chapter 14: Toxic Positivity and the NFT Echo Chamber

Questions that would be entirely mundane in any other investment forum — what has the team accomplished, what assets do they possess, why should anyone trust they can deliver on their promises — are treated as hostile.

The stark reality is that there aren't answers.

Party Ape Billionaire Club is just as insubstantial, yet they superficially succeeded, so there's an incentive to uphold the collective illusion.

This is amplified by an internal form of performative etiquette.

Participants ritualistically exchange good morning and good night wishes, condensed into the shorthand GM and GN.

While this may seem trivial, there's nothing inherently suspicious about saying good morning or good night, but in practice, it's a distinct ritual, not merely a shibboleth, but a repetitive act that signals in-group membership and affirms loyalty continuously.

If you possess Diamond Hands, it means you're willing to hold a token until some promised future where the value goes to the moon; you're not a Paper Hands loser who gets easily spooked by instability, volatility, or the fact that there's no reason to believe anyone will ever want to buy a Crypto Astronut in the future.

The shorthand WAGMI, We're All Going To Make It, is casually thrown around even in openly zero-sum competitions where, by definition, most participants will explicitly not make it.

But you can't point that out because that would be FUD.

And if you're spreading FUD, then you're NGMI, Not Going to Make It.

And making it, getting rich, is all that counts.

HFSP, have fun staying poor.

These ideas are synthesized into a No True Scotsman paradigm. The "we" in We're All Going To Make It doesn't refer to everyone; it refers to the select few, the chosen, the Diamond Hands and the hodlers.

Those who succeed are clearly the We, and if you didn't succeed, then you weren't part of it.

Individuals who express anger over being scammed by a rug-pull, malware, or social engineering are ridiculed and belittled for not following the crowd.

This cultivates a community conditioned to ignore warning signs and dismiss criticism, a community with internal language and customs that are explicitly incompatible with outside dialogue.

Skepticism is FUD from non-believers attempting to undermine the value of your assets and manipulate a crash or trick you into being a paper hands.

It all aligns with narratives of sin and deception, a chosen few who are privileged with advance knowledge about the promised land, which they can achieve by adhering to the rituals and expelling all doubt.

The end result is a self-organizing high-control group.

And the consequences of that are clear: there are still individuals convinced that somehow someone will resurrect the remnants of Evolved Apes and fulfill the rest of the project, a belief founded on no observable evidence.

So the question then becomes, what do the tokens actually accomplish?

Chapter 15: The Limitations of NFT Functionality

As previously mentioned, the token itself is just a container for a bit of data.

Now, this container is exceedingly small, to the extent that even an average cellphone photograph is several times too large to fit.

Due to the nature of the chain, updating software placed onto the chain is both challenging and costly.

Complicated programs must be divided into multiple tokens, each containing a smart contract defining a portion of the whole, and all of these contracts need to interlink and reference each other, while considering that each transaction that computes or alters information incurs processing fees; only reading information is free.

The process of fixing a bug in a smart contract essentially involves minting a new copy of the contract and then navigating various steps to rename the old and new contracts so that the new copy bears the name that any other interacting contracts are seeking, incurring fees for nearly every step of that process.

This creates an amusing Catch-22 where, on one hand, there's the insistence that the NFTs that end users acquire are potentially extremely powerful, capable of being miniature self-governing applets that exist in a network of similar applets, while on the other hand, there's a substantial motivation to invest as little as possible into them.

For instance, Wolf Game was a somewhat popular NFT-based gambling game that boasted about being wholly hosted on-chain, at great cost.

Everything from the pixel art wolves and sheep to the game's coding was stored on Ethereum.

The premise of the game is that users would mint a character token, which had a 90% chance of being a sheep and a 10% chance of being a wolf, with a finite supply of wolves and sheep available.

The key point here is that the character tokens weren't just a piece of art and a serial number, but tiny programs that allowed users to perform actions like staking.

The issue is that their code was riddled with multiple bugs, and since some of those bugs were embedded in the character tokens, they were replicated across all 13,809 minted tokens.

A malfunctioning token can't be patched; it must be replaced.

Thus, the Wolf Game developers were compelled to not only redeploy all their contracts but also attempt to remint and distribute identical copies of every token created.

It didn't go smoothly.

Chapter 16: The Role of Wallet Managers

Given the risks inherent in embedding functionality within the token itself, and the high cost of interaction, the most common application is to use external systems simply to check for token ownership.

This introduces another player into the ecosystem: wallet managers like MetaMask.

In just a few short years, the system has become so bloated and complex that it has necessitated the development of middleware applications that simplify the process of creating wallets, switching wallets, and mediating interactions between the wallet and external systems.

From one perspective, these wallet managers are the golden key that makes everything function.

They resolve the single-sign-on issue, allowing your web browser to seamlessly recognize that it's you using it, automatically negotiating permissions based on relevant tokens.

It's your login, your credit card, your Steam profile, and your bank account all consolidated into a single point of contact, making interactions with Web3, the internet of the future, frictionless.

From another viewpoint, it's a massive point of failure that holds so much information, so many permissions, and so much value that it becomes an exceedingly obvious target, created by individuals who claim to be building a security product in 2021 that doesn't obfuscate key phrases within the UI or utilize two-factor authentication.

Remember, once again, that these individuals intend to place medical records, driver's licenses, professional certifications, and real estate deeds into their system.

They should not be trusted.

The entire market is riddled with scams, and has been since Bitcoin first gained traction.

Every conceivable scam structure has been dusted off and redeployed in this explicitly unregulated market where victims largely lack recourse.

These range from institutional scams, such as Ponzi schemes, pump and dumps, and insider trading, to mid-level scams like gold brick schemes and wash trading, to grittier scams like phishing and fake links.

Pump and dumps, in particular, are executed in broad daylight, as it's not illegal; it simply violates the terms of service of the exchanges utilized, so the worst-case scenario is that you lose your account.

They'll straightforwardly guide you through the process of executing a pump and dump, no codewords, diagrams and all.

They're notable as they represent a two-headed scam because you might get recruited onto the pump side of the scheme, or you might think you're being recruited to pump, but you're actually the dump.

As previously noted, blockchain is resistant to direct man-in-the-middle attacks, where someone tries to inject false data directly onto the chain, but man-in-the-middle attacks are infrequent.

In an environment like cryptocurrency, with few, if any, repercussions for misconduct that remains within the cryptosphere, man-in-the-middle attacks are entirely unnecessary.

Why bother brute-forcing your false data onto the chain when you can deceive someone into granting you access to their wallet and then transfer all their assets out?

Every smart contract becomes a self-rewarding bug bounty where the payout is whatever apes and coins you can snatch before anyone notices.

And that doesn't even touch on the topic of malware!

Smart contracts are just code; they're software, so there's no reason they can't function as viruses or worms; the primary limitation is processing power.

Moreover, it's a virus that someone can directly insert into your bankless bank account and simply wait for you to activate it.

And, yes, that's correct; there's no offer/confirmation step in transferring tokens, so someone who knows your wallet can just drop items right into it, so, like, remember that.

The most amusing aspect of this is that the whole ecosystem operates on the strict assumption that possession equates to ownership and access equals permission, which is absolutely wild coming from software developers who claim to be very concerned with system security.

If someone tricked you into transferring your Bored Ape, it's now theirs.

The only mechanism in the system for differentiating legitimate transactions from illegitimate ones is the consensus mechanism, which is solely focused on whether or not the transactions adhered to the software's rules.

The only illegitimacy it acknowledges comes from individuals trying to insert fake data.

When you are tricked into doing something, all the mechanics that follow are, by the system's rules, legitimate.

It's a legal transfer.

More relevant, however, is the sheer prevalence of these scams.

The one market that cryptocurrency has successfully disrupted is the fraud market.

Consider this: a large population of individuals has willingly self-identified as having significant disposable income, poor judgment, low social awareness, a high tolerance for nonsensical risk, and being highly suggestible.

Individuals who fall victim to these scams essentially have no options other than taking to social media and attempting to stir up enough of a frenzy to convince marketplaces like OpenSea to act as de facto censors by delisting stolen tokens.

There's no authority to which you can report them that has the power to restore your tokens; your best hope is to deny the scammers profit on their incredibly low-cost operations.

If your business involves deceiving individuals out of their money, you would be foolish not to seize the opportunity.

Not only have participants highlighted their vulnerability to incoherent promises of future returns, but the immutable structure of the chain, the persistence of data, and the ease with which that data can be compiled mean that for scammers, it's exceedingly straightforward to find targets.

Every Discord for a rug-pull NFT project is a roster of potential victims. The ledger of BAYC holders is a shopping list of targets. The Twitter account of anyone complaining about what they lost on Evolved Apes is the low-hanging fruit of a very ripe orchard.

And that serves as a perfect segue into privacy concerns!

Chapter 17: Privacy Concerns in the Blockchain

A low-trust environment is also a low-privacy environment.

Anything you do on a blockchain is, by design, accessible to anyone who knows how to navigate the data.

Now, you might be wondering, isn't that the opposite of how it's supposed to function?

I thought crypto was supposed to be anonymous?

So, yes, crypto is anonymous by default; there's no intrinsic requirement for proof of identity, and in fact, numerous applications that would benefit from a stricter one-to-one correlation between accounts and individuals struggle with this.

On forums and social media, it's referred to as sockpuppeting; in crypto, it's termed a Sybil attack, where users can create numerous alternate identities by generating additional accounts or wallets.

The wash trading epidemic on OpenSea relies on the ability to pretend you're several different people while buying apes from yourself for hundreds of thousands of dollars.

Rather than being anonymous, this is pseudonymous.

Everyone can see which wallets and contracts your wallet interacts with based on long hash addresses like this, but that hash is only implicitly tied to your identity based on circumstantial connections.

Of course, a significant circumstantial connection would be registering with a crypto-based social auction platform that intrinsically links the two.

This makes it relatively easy to observe that Laina Morris, Overly Attached Girlfriend, spent $153 on March 31st to mint the Overly Attached Girlfriend NFT, followed by a $205 reserve on April 2nd to list the NFT on Foundation.

Ethereum whale Farzin Fardin Fard then purchased the token on April 3rd for 200 Ethereum, of which 30 went to Foundation, leaving Laina with the remaining 170, which she converted into USD using the exchange service Kraken in a block of 105 on April 4th and a block of 65 on April 22nd, accumulating a combined payout of $374,726.

After her sale, Zoe Roth exchanged the Ethereum for dollars via Coinbase the following day and hasn't interacted with the wallet since.

Kyle Craven minted several other tokens but mostly just divided the Ethereum from the initial sale into two separate holding wallets where it has remained untouched since.

You don't need to be a super hacker to figure this out; it's all publicly accessible; that's the entire point of the system.

And in another feature-not-bug situation, remember that nothing can be deleted from the blockchain without immense effort.

Now, that's fine if the blockchain only contains a contextually relevant log of transactions; there are certainly contexts where such transparency is desirable, but it falls apart when discussing using the blockchain itself as the storage medium for, say, an entire social network.

Blockchain-based social network Scuttlebutt seems to be somewhat aware that this is a bad idea, as if somewhere within their human brains they recognize it might be a mistake to make it impossible to remove things from the system when they warn users that anyone willing to dig can uncover any old usernames, photos, and bios, but that doesn't deter them.

So, if someone posts, say, child abuse imagery, revenge porn, your home address, intimate details of your private life, there's simply nothing you can really do about it.

If you accidentally overshare, posting information you maybe shouldn't have, it's already too late.

You can attempt to hide it, but you can't erase it.

Remember that if someone knows your wallet address, they can drop tokens directly into it?

As previously mentioned, there's an entire scam where you send someone an NFT that uses lifted art from who cares, but the smart contract is malicious code that drains their wallet if they ever engage with it to move, sell, stake, or burn it; it just becomes a landmine sitting in their wallet indefinitely.

Even on the non-malware side of things, people have already been utilizing this to dump promotional tokens into the wallets of celebrities and influencers, but, you know, explicit content is an "any second now" kind of threat, right?

"Oh, look, I minted a photo of your front door and dropped it directly into your wallet."

And you can't simply delete it; you need to actively send it somewhere and pay gas fees to do so.

Revolutionary new forms of harassment.

The end result here is a massive power imbalance that's ingrained in how you engage with this new world order.

Users who interact with the system authentically as themselves expose vast amounts of information about their identities and activities, while users who engage disingenuously are empowered in their capacity to deceive, defraud, and disappear.

Much of this rhetoric arises from a profound failure to grasp what a central authority truly is, or that you can decentralize data storage while centralizing data.

Ethereum is ultimately a central platform, and the fact that a handful of individuals must approve every major change before it can be executed is largely meaningless and symbolic, with the validation network ultimately existing somewhere between consortium and cartel.

Every large platform has multiple internal and external stakeholders that form a consensus regarding the direction of the platform.

Windows is not a single-minded monolith.

Apple issues voting shares.

Google is essentially a hydra.

While the network of Ethereum miners and validators isn't a formal corporation yet, there's no mechanism in place that compels them to act in the interest of users, particularly those who are poor and disempowered, where their interests conflict with their own.

The transition of Ethereum from proof of work to proof of stake has been vapourware largely because the validators simply opt not to.

Because proof of work, volatility, and high gas fees benefit them in the present, while proof of stake and low gas fees only serve to benefit them in a hypothetical future.

Because these glaring pitfalls arise when you allow individuals like Vitalik Buterin and Elon Musk to design the future.

The sole protection for Ethereum users is that the system is so cumbersome that all but the most egregious breaches aren't worth addressing.

Of course, this in reality means that only the wealthy have access to justice within the system.

If you consolidate all these various facets—your identity, your economic activities, the video games you play, the groups you join—into a single system, that constitutes a central system.

It doesn't matter how many different servers that system spans or how many validators must agree before changes can be implemented; you've pooled all that data in one location.

The proposed web3, crypto-driven future of the internet is a privacy catastrophe.

This is why I find MetaMask to be a terrifying product.

It's a container that's requesting you to pour unfathomable amounts of data and permissions into it.

It stands as a tremendous and monumental point of failure.

And this is where NFTs truly flourish into their ultimate form.

Chapter 18: NFTs as Access Passes

The primary purpose of tokens beyond speculation, ultimately, is to serve as access passes.

From a web engineering standpoint, envision tokens that are the ultimate cookies and consider a tracking token that users not only willingly associate with but eagerly drag along from device to device, ensuring continuity of tracking across all web activities.

The future version of the web, built upon cryptocurrency and mediated by financialized tokens, is a dystopia.

It's a technology designed to convert everything into money, to treat every aspect of our social existence as a marketplace, to attach an abstract, representative token to everything from video games to labor unions.

Now, proponents of Web3 will disagree with this viewpoint, particularly the assertion that cryptocurrency is inherent to Web3 and the two are inseparable, but that's the practical reality of the situation.

Every substantial project branding itself under the banner of Web3 is tethered to a blockchain, whether by issuing governance tokens, relying on the chain's smart contract layer, or necessitating possession of cryptocurrency to pay mandatory processing fees for participation.

They are at this point philosophically and technologically intertwined.

Less accessible, less free, less engaging, and significantly more expensive, Web3 is the forefront of a million paywalls and oppressive "code-enforced" DRM schemes marketed to idealists as a decentralized system where they, and not wealthy stakeholders, hold the power.

I perceive significant blind spots in a community that has spent so long fixating on the hype of an untenable fantasy Metaverse where they're the ones intimidating corporations with immutable ownership, ensuring their ability to resell video game horse armor, that they've failed to consider that the "enforcement of ownership" can and will be wielded against them if and when corporations choose to exploit their power in this realm.

The delusion among evangelists is that a tokenized economy where digital goods are mediated by NFTs would grant them more power, that items like digital games would have genuine ownership, encapsulated in the ability to be resold, but there's no reason to believe that this is how things would unfold.

The far more likely outcome is that tokens are utilized to constrain products even tighter.

Chapter 19: The Squid Game Token Scam

The Squid Game token scam is illustrative here.

In early November 2021, a new meme token emerged, inspired by the hit Netflix show Squid Game.

Over about a week, the token's price was inflated from a few cents to nearly $3000 USD.

Estimates suggest that the Squid developers netted approximately $3.38 million before liquidating their holdings, deleting their social media accounts, and vanishing without a trace.

A classic rug pull, but the truly remarkable detail is that it left buyers with not just a worthless token but a token that couldn't be sold at all.

Built into SQUID was a stipulation that in order to transfer or sell the tokens, a corresponding number of MARBLES tokens needed to be spent simultaneously.

The trick was that MARBLES were never available.

No rules were violated in this scam, and indeed the SQUID tokens function precisely as promised.

If you possess the requisite amount of MARBLES tokens, you can indeed transfer or sell your SQUID.

Just, good luck acquiring any.

A game developer can, in myriad ways, fulfill the promise of a "truly owned" digital token that becomes untradeable in practice, all while adhering to the rules.

Rules must always be evaluated for their capacity to oppress.

This is a blind spot for crypto enthusiasts because they simply assume they're the early adopters, the ones who will wield power, the ones who will establish the rules, and they're the ones who will engage in oppression.

Consider that any token capable of granting access can also be used to revoke it.

For instance, let's say I create a hangout spot on one of the Metaverse contender platforms, Decentraland, and we name it the Ahegao Alpaca Oasis.

The Oasis has a back room that only allows registered players to enter, meaning you need to have your MetaMask linked to Decentraland to gain access.

This type of gate is typically employed to create VIP areas, places where only individuals who hold a specific token or class of token can enter.

Only people with official Ahegao Alpacas can enter. But, as is well-known within the lore of the Metaverse, the Ahegao Alpacas have been at war with the Bored Ape Yacht Club for some time, so rather than verifying for an Alpaca token, I check for Ape tokens and subsequently deny entry.

Or perhaps I artificially inflate the difficulty for them, or raise my prices.

Now imagine that instead of running a hangout spot in a video game, I'm a Decentralized Finance organization offering mortgages in cryptocurrency, and I scrutinize your transaction history for donations to the NAACP as part of my "risk assessment protocol."

Imagine that Nestlé can monitor unionization efforts in real-time because the union is issuing governance tokens on a publicly auditable blockchain.

The belief that the world will be fairer if the rules are enshrined in code, enforced by computers, and rendered extremely difficult to change or circumvent is laughable.

It's not just naive but categorically ahistoric.

This is where much of my resistance originates.

You can create specialized crypto chains that have a negligible environmental impact, but the force of that model is culturally destructive.

The existing system is flawed, but this is merely a worse version of the current system.

It doesn't even end there.

It's tokens all the way down.

Chapter 20: Play-to-Earn Games and the Axie Infinity Case

"This game has a high barrier of entry, so most people can't participate unless they have what's termed a scholarship, where someone essentially covers their entry costs to allow them to play the game, and then they can split the profits afterward."

For instance, Axie Infinity is a so-called "play to earn" video game based on Ethereum, but because Ethereum is too slow and costly to interact with directly, the developers, Sky Mavis, created a side-chain called Ronin, which consists of a governance currency called AXS, the game character tokens called Axies, and the in-game currency called Smooth Love Potions, or SLP.

All these components are designed to function as money because that's the objective of the machine.

The so-called play-to-earn model serves as a great case study in what the end result of the crypto ecosystem actually looks like.

Axie Infinity receives a great deal of credulous media coverage as a handful of people in the Philippines manage to make a marginal living by playing the game and trading their SLP, which allows Sky Mavis to present themselves as a humanitarian organization rather than a for-profit business profiting off all the individuals rushing to purchase a team of Axies in the belief they can earn simply by playing.

Now, to be brief, Axie Infinity is a lightweight card-based PvP game where players battle using a team of three creatures called Axies.

It's a bit like Pokémon and a bit like Slay the Spire.

Axies possess randomized attributes and are all tokenized, so selling an Axie means you're selling that specific Axie.

Smooth Love Potions are used for breeding Axies, thereby forming the foundation of the economy as they are fungible in comparison to the Axies themselves.

Matches can be ranked or unranked, but only ranked matches, entered using energy that recharges daily, can earn SLP.

The amount of energy available depends on the number of Axies in your wallet, ranging from 20 to 60.

Additionally, higher-ranked matches yield more SLP.

Greater amounts of SLP mean a larger stable of Axies, which translates into more energy to play matches, greater flexibility within the metagame, superior team compositions, and generally better stats, leading to easier victories.

Thus, the earning potential disparity between higher and lower-ranked accounts is quite significant.

What coverage tends to highlight and then quickly gloss over is that the game is extremely expensive to enter, costing hundreds of dollars to assemble a basic team, leading to the emergence of what are euphemistically referred to as scholarship programs: businesses like Whale Scholars that establish numerous accounts, grant players access to the game account but not the underlying wallet, and then pay players a share of the SLP the account generates.

Whale Scholars, along with other "mentorship" businesses, retain full control of the wallet, and thus the Axies, the SLP, and any AXS.

It's capitalism in its purest form.

Players invest their time grinding for SLP, and then the owners take a portion of the returns.

Players barely manage to earn minimum wage while the owners, who take 50% from dozens or even hundreds of players, are free to speculate on digital land.

"Look what the Whale Scholars just acquired. We have land in the Arctic, baby! We have Arctic land!"

Axie's energy system is fundamentally flawed in how it promotes this very middleman arrangement.

If you have 21 Axies in your wallet, you can create one account that has 60 energy at its disposal, or you can set up seven bare-minimum accounts with 20 energy each.

A high-ranked account with 60 energy will dramatically outperform a single low-ranked account with 20 energy, but seven accounts that are played daily by others present far superior ROI because it requires virtually no effort beyond collecting your share.

Even more tellingly, between August and October 2021, the internal economy of Axie Infinity collapsed.

Not to absolute rock bottom, but enough that nearly all but the top-ranking players fell below the average daily wage in the Philippines, with low-ranked players dropping below minimum wage.

Naavik, a think tank and consulting firm that conducts comprehensive research on game economies, has performed an in-depth analysis of the Axie economy, identifying the core issue as psychological: players aren't playing for enjoyment; they're playing to earn.

They approach the game as a job, leading to little interest in game items for their own merit.

Once they accumulate enough assets to cover their job, they cease reinvesting and begin cashing out.

The price of low-quality Axies, which new players are likely to purchase to onboard at the lowest cost, is propped up solely by players buying them at a rate roughly equal to their generation.

This necessitates either mentors scaling up their teams by purchasing Axies instead of generating them or new players introducing fresh capital into the ecosystem through onboarding.

However, as more players engage, more SLP and Axies will be generated, resulting in a fundamentally unsustainable economic model where an infinite influx of new players must continuously enter the ecosystem to maintain stable pricing.

If it tips one way or the other, you either face runaway inflation or runaway deflation.

This is a common occurrence in games; games constantly disrupt their internal economies, it usually just doesn't matter because you're dealing with completely fictional currency, gems, or dragon bones.

A genuinely stable economy isn't even desirable from a gameplay perspective, in any case.

Gentle inflation ultimately aids newer and more casual players by lowering costs in the in-game economy, allowing those players to participate and have fun.

Of course, if your pitch is "play to earn" rather than "play for enjoyment," where the optics bolstering your company's fictitious valuation rely entirely on the premise that players can indeed earn, this creates a very different incentive structure, doesn't it?

More individuals engage with Axie Infinity to attempt to profit than to play simply because they enjoy it.

This is a fundamental flaw in the model.

If you market your game based on earning potential, you will attract individuals aiming to industrialize your platform faster and in greater numbers than would otherwise engage.

This is precisely the parasitic situation that games have been actively minimizing for decades because it produces vicious negative externalities.

If players can sell their in-game items, it alters how they approach the game; it changes how they optimize their playtime.

Since the overwhelming majority of games are openly a non-investment—a straightforward exchange of money for entertainment, also referred to as a "purchase"—players typically optimize their playtime for intangible returns such as enjoyment, distraction, socialization, relaxation, challenge, achievement, and narrative fulfillment, with absolutely no expectation that the money and time invested should yield anything beyond those experiences.

The key shift here, and the meaningless buzz phrase you'll encounter online, is the assertion that the outcomes of playing a game should "retain value," which is code for having a potentially speculative price.

To keep the grift mill running for a few more months, Sky Mavis has adjusted the economy to decrease the amount of SLP players can earn per hour.

It's a nightmarishly thin edge to navigate, and the primary outcome has been the establishment of an entire tier of pit bosses running teams of players grinding out Smooth Love Potions.

And, like all bosses, they haven't taken the downturn in stride but have instead started cracking the whip.

> "We do not accept mediocre gaming anymore. You need to generate at least 120-150 SLP a day, and those yielding more will be rewarded with additional percentages. I prioritize those with gaming experience; we have a separate program for charity."

Evangelists often point to this as inspiring, highlighting people in economically disadvantaged countries managing to make a meager living from merely playing a video game.

I reject that narrative. It's horrific.

Chapter 21: The Dystopian Reality of the Play-to-Earn Model

Our global system is so fundamentally unjust that individuals are congratulating themselves for creating a whole new type of online UwU pit boss who admonishes you to grind harder or face termination, but caps it off with blushy emojis.

Oopsie, looks like someone didn't meet their quota.

This situation is dismal.

I believe the aspect that casual observers don't grasp about NFT enthusiasts is their dedication, the staggering amount of capital they already control, and how deeply entrenched they are in the culture of the individuals operating the platforms we utilize daily, and that alone is a compelling reason for people to pay attention.

They possess substantial resources and influence that they can leverage to try and make Fetch happen.

This serves as a pivotal point. Essentially, the future will unfold in one of two broad scenarios.

One possibility is that some new technological buzzword emerges, causing "blockchain" and "web3" to lose their allure among investors, the influx of new buyers ceases, and the early investors cash out as best they can, ultimately bursting the entire bubble.

The alternative is that they succeed, and cryptocurrency manages to force its way into enough areas of our lives that it becomes inescapable; we are all compelled in some manner to maintain a crypto wallet to handle whatever coins and tokens become necessary for participation in society, granting early investors a captive audience and a steady flow of capital.

To quote German sociotechnologist Jürgen Geuter, better known by his online persona Tante:

"There are aspects of your digital life that you currently can't really sell, but that's what they want to change. Everything needs to be bought and sold; everything is simply a vehicle for more speculation. The reason they want you to be able to resell your access token to some service (instead of buying or renting it as we do today) is to create even more markets for speculation, and the smart contracts can be configured in such a way that they profit at every turn."

The assertions that this technology enables an immutable ledger of ownership are themselves largely hollow posturing, even from within the ecosystem.

Remember that most of the actual items being referenced are not stored within the chains themselves, as the chains are too slow, restrictive, and ineffective for that purpose, and because many of the items being sold are purely ephemeral.

The IPFS address for any given media token can be effortlessly minted onto another competing chain, or even the same chain. That's not even right-click saving; that's referencing the exact same media.

What makes the token on Ethereum more authoritative than the token on Tezos, Cardano, Solana, Ergo, Celo, Binance, Algorand, Polkadot, EOS, Tron, VeChain, Ethereum Classic, Fantom, Stellar, Stacks, Neo, Waves, Holo, LINK, Radix, Harmony, Oasis, ICON, Secret, IOTA, Crown, TERA, Omni, Enigma, Elastos, Edgeware, Bytom, or Fuse?

If a chain hard forks, which version of your assets is the genuine one?

Bitcoin is, itself, entangled in a turf war between Bitcoin, Bitcoin Cash, and Bitcoin SV.

The notion of unchangeable ownership dictated by these systems relies on a singular champion.

In truth, your NFTs within the Ethereum ecosystem are ultimately as confined, isolated, and insignificant as your Steam trading cards.

You might encounter protocols like Polygon that claim to facilitate the transfer of assets across different chains, but that's merely a trick.

It's impossible to extract something from a chain; all they actually accomplish is generating a new token at the target location and appending a note to the original token that reads, "I'm currently elsewhere, please don't transfer or sell me."

This request is regulated by smart contracts, which are susceptible to poor coding.

In gaming terms, they would be swiftly scrutinized for item duplication flaws, a vulnerability that is essentially unavoidable in a widespread adoption scenario.

It's a system that is both unyielding and fragile, and this setup disproportionately benefits the unscrupulous.

One of the complexities is that it is nearly impossible to disentangle the digital scarcity principles of NFTs from cryptocurrency and the fundamental ideologies upon which cryptocurrency was founded.

One emerged from the other, and they are essentially forever intertwined.

One of the ironies in all of this is that any genuine artistic or anti-capitalist applications of the underlying technology depend on it remaining niche.

At a fundamental level, the systems are simply inadequate, being slow, complicated to navigate, and generally convoluted. For the most part, to the extent that they are usable at all, it is largely due to having only a handful of users.

There are blockchains that are relatively responsive and affordable because they lack popularity.

Hic Et Nunc is a well-regarded art marketplace on the Tezos blockchain. Currently, transaction fees and inflation are quite low, allowing many transactions to occur in the range of five to twenty dollars, but this situation exists because it sits at 45th in terms of popularity—just sufficient to have actual users but not high enough to attract excessive bots.

If Tezos experiences a surge in popularity, as they say, everything changes.

Users flock to the platform in a manner that outpaces the number of validators, the value of Tez soars, and the real marketplace for Hic Et Nunc users encounters hyperinflation, where currency hoarders are rewarded generously while buyers face penalties.

Chapter 22: Deflation and Its Impact

Alright, we need to pause here for a moment because this is genuinely important but exceedingly complex, akin to textbook-level subject matter, so here's the condensed version.

Deflation is counter-intuitive because the line is rising, which makes it appear beneficial, but it's only advantageous if you already possess the currency. As the purchasing power of a currency increases — typically because cash becomes scarcer — the prices of goods and services decrease.

A deflationary economy penalizes purchases, as anything you acquire today will inevitably be cheaper in the future.

If you need to buy items that aren't financial assets — things that don't appreciate in value, like food, clothing, rent, vehicles, or transit fares — you end up hurting yourself.

This is hyperdeflation, and it's not only built into cryptocurrencies with their capped total coin supply but is also viewed as desirable by their creators and advocates.

This is what "going to the moon" signifies.

Now let's discuss unions.

Utilizing tokens to authenticate union membership and engage in union activities relies on the technology being obscure enough that union busters and their clients don't perceive it as a significant area to monitor.

Also, that ship has already sailed.

Union busters and gig economy proponents adore crypto; they embrace DeFi, smart contracts, and NFTs.

And why wouldn't they?

It's an environment that dismantles consumer protections and transfers significant amounts of explicit power to the affluent.

In many respects, this is merely a framework for deferring trust to machines and pretending that there aren't human actors involved, and if there's one thing union busters cherish, it's the possibility of an unbreakable individual contract whose injustices can all be attributed to a machine.

The current state of the web, concentrated within a few mega platforms, results from accumulating complexity.

We once had a web where anyone could learn to create a webpage in HTML in just one afternoon.

It merely involved writing text and then using tags to format that text.

However, over time, people understandably desired the web to be more functional and aesthetically pleasing, leading to the expansion of possibilities through scripting languages that enabled dynamic, interactive content.

Soon, the definition of what constituted a "website" and how it looked became unreachable for casual users, eventually moving beyond the grasp of all but the most devoted hobbyists.

It became the realm of specialists. Casual users, excluded by complexity, gravitated towards templates, services, and platforms.

This process gradually concentrated a critical mass of users within a handful of social media platforms.

Even within that space, new power structures are already emerging.

Significant amounts of capital and power are consolidating in companies like Consensys, which owns MetaMask, and Animoca Brands, which has extensive investments in crypto gaming.

OpenSea, the currently dominant marketplace for tokens across various chains, is fulfilling the power roles users require.

While the chain itself is theoretically the arbiter of truth, nothing prevents individuals from populating the chain with falsehoods, creating a demand not only for a chain parser — a service that enables users to engage with the chain — but also an interpreter of the chain.

Motivational speaker and gullible target Calvin Baccera claimed to have lost three Bored Ape Yacht Club tokens to a social engineering scam.

In response, he took to Twitter to rally a mob that could pressure OpenSea and two other marketplaces into marking the tokens as stolen and preventing their sale.

Calvin ultimately regained his tokens by paying a ransom, which is really the only recourse available, and he doesn't seem to recognize that, from the thieves' perspective, this is a wholly desirable outcome.

They succeeded. Their scheme worked.

This occurs frequently.

Bored Ape members are particularly vulnerable to fraud due to their unique blend of greed and low social awareness.

In an attempt to avoid paying platform fees and royalties, many of them shifted from OpenSea to conduct transactions on a dubious platform called NFT Trader, which allowed scammers to execute a simple link swap scam, resulting in the theft of at least a dozen different ape tokens within a few days.

The crux of Calvin's situation lies in how the platforms interacting with the chain are being assigned by users to serve as the de facto authority, not on what the chain states, but on what the chain signifies.

It merely replicates existing power hierarchies within the new environment.

This is where advocates assert that the solution lies in DAOs—decentralized autonomous organizations—a "revolutionary" new method to organize individuals that will facilitate the decentralized governance of these systems.

So that's the claim, but what is it, precisely, once you strip away the embellishments?

A DAO constitutes an organization whose membership, roles, and privileges are determined by the ownership of relevant tokens on a specific blockchain, as well as the underlying software that carries out relevant operations.

And that's essentially it.

To clarify, a conceptual DAO consists of three components: people, a digital machine comprised of smart contracts, and a token that enables the people to interact with the machine.

In practice, most entities claiming to be DAOs lack the machine entirely, and a significant number either do not possess the token or only have the token.

The advantage of a DAO is that it simplifies the formation of a formal organization at theoretically any scale, from a couple of individuals to large groups of stakeholders, and the programming layer allows for automation of certain activities and outcomes.

If the organization votes through the DAO interface, the results of that vote are automatically recorded and potentially executed.

However, that perspective is misleading.

As with tokens themselves, a DAO has no inherent functionality; it's merely a container for code.

I might as well be referring to all the possibilities available with a webpage.

As previously mentioned, many organizations portraying themselves as DAOs have no machine functionality whatsoever.

It's commonplace to encounter a DAO that has issued a governance token—the script used for voting—while the systems to actually utilize that token are relegated to some vague future timeline in the roadmap.

That open-endedness is crucial because, while the assertion is that these machines will further democratize the internet, the technical complexity they introduce and the new specialized programming skills they necessitate concentrate considerable power in the hands of those who can create the templates that enable non-programmers to engage with it.

It merely plants the seeds for the eventual reestablishment of the status quo.

The Facebook/Google/Amazon-dominated internet emerged because the technical costs of building a modern website surpassed what the vast majority of amateurs could handle, so everyone shifted to templates, then to services, and ultimately to platforms.

This doesn't even reset the timeline; the technical expenses associated with creating a DAO are already far beyond any casual amateur, partly because all of this is engineered by programmers and partly due to the stakes involved.

The only true utility of this technology lies in managing on-chain assets.

A DAO program can monitor the state of the chain and interact with it, enabling DAO members to vote on the fate of those assets, after which the DAO program can automatically execute the decisions.

However, this raises the stakes.

Because a DAO can directly observe and interact with on-chain assets, there's a risk that through flawed programming or unforeseen vulnerabilities, a malicious actor could exploit a DAO to access various resources.

The risk is directly proportional to the value of the assets stored on-chain, and remember, again, that advocates wish to place everything on-chain.

The amusing truth is that this scenario has already unfolded before.

In fact, it occurred with the very first DAO ever created, known as The DAO.

This entire saga transpired over three months in 2016, from April to June.

The DAO was an Ethereum-based venture capital fund that sought to utilize code to establish an investment firm without a conventional management structure or board of directors, a scheme framed as "lightweight" and "reducing bureaucratic overhead," but in reality, it merely translated to an effort to minimize human accountability for the fund's actions and conduct.

This unprecedented manifestation of greed excited the major speculative players in Ethereum, so much so that during the presale in April and May, they funneled 14% of the entire ether volume into The DAO's central wallet.

Now, because The DAO's underlying code was open-source, both experts and malicious individuals could scrutinize it for weaknesses, and indeed, vulnerabilities were discovered.

However, because, at the end of the day, flesh-and-blood humans are the ones actually clicking buttons and making decisions, the actual leadership of the nominally-leaderless DAO, eager for wealth and recognition, opted to launch in late May regardless.

Three weeks later, The DAO's programming was exploited, and the attacker managed to transfer one-third of The DAO's funds into a holding wallet, roughly 5% of the entire Ethereum economy, valued at the time between 16 and 17 million dollars.

Chapter 23: The DAO Illusion

Now, because this jeopardized the financial interests of capital holders, the Ethereum project as a whole was almost immediately forked to reverse the hack and safeguard the wealthy's interests.

Ethereum Classic, the branch of the fork that didn't reverse the attack, continues to exist today, though it's notably less popular despite being demonstrably more principled.

Because all the rhetoric surrounding "decentralization" is a deception.

It's merely words.

Ultimately, the individuals in control—the ones who constructed the system to serve their interests—remain in control and keep a killswitch at hand.

Crypto is hardly a decade old, and organizations deemed too big to fail already exist.

The entire debacle revealed the truth from the outset: labeling a DAO as a revolutionary structure is smoke and mirrors; it's simply voting shares.

You might as well refer to Apple as "a bold experiment in democracy" since a baker's dozen of individuals make the decisions instead of just one.

Regardless of future pitfalls, DAOs are also severely limited.

They are, once again, just code.

While advocates assert that they can reinvent social organization, mentally consider all the issues, conflicts, and decision-making challenges that social organizations face, and ask how many of those can actually be resolved through code.

Some can easily be translated into computer programs.

Automated bookkeeping, payouts, collections, data tracking—sure, those are all functions organizations can conceptually utilize.

But how do you program for the fact that Red simply doesn't get along with Blue?

The sales pitch promises organizations bound by unbreakable rules, but how many organizations genuinely benefit from that level of rigidity?

Particularly, what happens when the version of the rules enforced by code encounters a complication that the programmers didn't foresee?

What occurs if someone with legitimate stakes in the DAO begins spamming the organization's internal systems with malicious requests?

What if not enough participants engage in voting?

What if the system locks itself up?

What if the rules are manipulated?

What if the system commits a crime?

Chapter 24: The Limitations of DAOs

If this technology were to achieve mass adoption, a future time bomb already exists in the fact that very few of these systems have accounted for mortality in their structural considerations, because "what if someone with an important token dies?" is an easily overlooked issue when you're an insulated tech bro who reimagines vending machines as Bodega Boxes.

Now, all these hypotheticals are technically solvable; you can design contingency systems to address them, but then you need to contemplate contingencies for those contingencies, because what if someone utilizes systems intended for managing deceased or absent members to expel individuals they simply dislike?

And again, you can only use code to enforce interactions that the programmers make enforceable through the code.

ConstitutionDAO, a hastily assembled initiative to bid on one of the few remaining original copies of the US Constitution, already encountered most of these problems as the project failed to win the auction and is now attempting to issue refunds — a task that the hastily constructed machine was never designed to handle.

The reality is that most organizations with any significant social complexity, even tiny entities like video game guilds, are too intricate to be accurately encapsulated in code.

There are too many contingencies and contingencies for those contingencies, and contingencies for those contingencies to account for, so rather than trying to translate social interactions into code, the DAO is relegated to only managing code-appropriate tasks, such as bookkeeping, digital signature verification, and on-chain asset management.

But that doesn't constitute a revolutionary new way to organize people; it's simply a productivity tool.

The DAO can establish a process for voting on actions, but the moment the outcomes of those actions transition off-chain—that is, into the real world—the DAO program is powerless.

The program cannot compel humans to execute the group's decisions; that remains an analog dilemma.

The entire operation quickly confronts an incentive barrier where it's simply faster and easier to resolve issues verbally, through abstract trust relationships and promises, to achieve the same results.

This is why it's so common for DAOs to lack any of the internal machinery that would genuinely transform them into what they claim to be: it's often just simpler not to.

Overall, DAOs are not some groundbreaking new model; they are a tool built alongside cryptocurrency that only offers meaningful advantages when interacting with cryptocurrency as a means for speculative trading and managing financial instruments.

The rest is merely a gimmick, a sluggish, inflexible tool for executing straw polls.

Once more, many of these ultimately boil down to a strategy to minimize liability on the part of the creators.

The creators of Inu Yasha Token, a meme coin DAO founded on nothing but the transient concept of the InuYasha anime, illustrated this well when they were confronted with copyright concerns, openly trading on a recognized brand explicitly for recognition.

Their response to the inquiry essentially boiled down to a misunderstanding of copyright, and an insistence that it didn't matter because no one is accountable—the DAO did it, no humans are responsible, just this nebulous sentient carbon cloud.

"You have a really good way to explain it about the um about the copyright issue that everyone's afraid of, because they don't want to invest in a token that's going to be told to cease and desist or..."

"Right, yeah, so I mean, to clear that up I think first you need to distinguish between a mark and a copy. Right? So right now on the website, it's all custom art done by Steven. Your friend Steven. So there is no copy. I mean, the only person that can really copyright us right now is Steven. Uh. You know?"

"What about logo likeness or character likeness?"

> *"Yeah, so trademarks. Um, it's possible that the InuYasha mark could become scrutinized. However, we're a decentralized autonomous organization officially, and the token is launched on the Ethereum blockchain, so there's really no going back. I'm just a community member. I'm not an owner; there's really no single entity that has ownership, so I mean it's on the blockchain now, there's no going back."*

And that bit perfectly encapsulates the mindset of many involved in these ventures.

They wanted to leverage the Inu Yasha brand for recognition but didn't want to seek permission because they likely would be denied, so they proceeded anyway, believing that now that it's "on chain," it can't be easily removed—so I suppose they just have to let them proceed?

"It's on the blockchain now, there's no going back."

Things take a humorous turn in that aggravating way when you encounter a DAO attempting to be legitimate, only to reveal that underneath, they're legally a co-op or an LLC or some other existing legal entity.

Unless your objective is a scam, there's nothing truly revolutionary about their structure or functionality.

Li Jin, the co-founder of several predatory venture capital firms that focus on polishing the image of the gig economy to distract from its erosion of labor, has an extended Twitter thread where she attempts to promote DAOs as the future of unions, though her reasoning is not only flimsy, relying heavily on magical thinking, but also sprinkled with inexplicable falsehoods.

For instance, she champions Yield Guild, a DAO she describes as "a gaming guild comprised of thousands of play-to-earn gamers. An onramp that brings more players into play-to-earn gaming, it can represent gamers & lobby game developers for better policies. Its scale also enables the collective to offer benefits and protections (e.g. healthcare, paid time off) that would be infeasible if gamers were operating independently."

This is a tremendous exaggeration of what Yield actually is. It's not a union, nor does it function as one, nor does it aspire to function as a union. It's not even a DAO, although it does have aspirations of transitioning into one. It's at best a somewhat decentralized cartel experimenting with extracting funds from players by gamifying their participation in the guild.

In practice, it is a Discord server that assists play-to-earn players in finding sponsorships, pivoting from one game to another, and generally complaining about how much they dislike their jobs.

In fact, in response to Li Jin's tweets, server members expressed this:

> "I've read that through the YGG DAO members can access healthcare—is this true? Is there more information available on this? Any way to learn about what is offered? Or is this still in development? As a freelancer, I'm always interested in exploring more options."

> "I actually don't know that, lol. It would be fantastic to partner with healthcare."

> "Where did you get that information? We haven't heard anything about it."

> "Hmm, yeah—I think Li used it as an example of potential benefits and didn't mean it literally, but nothing of that sort has been discussed yet."

Now, on a functional level, most DAOs utilize an administrative system based on the use and expenditure of internal scrip, the governance tokens.

There's a fair amount of variability in how they are employed, but essentially they operate either as proportional voting power, akin to voting shares in a publicly traded company, fiat voting power where possessing more than one token serves no purpose, or direct voting power where tokens are utilized to cast votes, and additional tokens can be expended for more votes.

Typically, this scrip can be purchased and sold, even on a secondary market, and possession of it is usually a defining component of membership.

Rather than structuring like a union, Yield's overt goal for their DAO is to function as a hedge fund, using the exchange value of their token as a means to gather resources for investment into play-to-earn games, and allowing Yield members to utilize their tokens to access these DAO-owned resources.

In fact, Yield is so distanced from the purpose and function of a union that its roadmap includes potentially implementing something called holographic consensus, which is a futures market where participants wager on which proposals will or won't be approved using their governance tokens as stakes. It's remarkable if you sought to construct a mechanism whose sole purpose is to gradually concentrate political power over time.

Additionally, many employ a proof-of-stake staking system to reward members with extra tokens, with no limit on how many tokens any single member can possess.

This entire arrangement creates a system where participants with only a few tokens are incentivized to not vote against the interests of heavily staked members, plus anything you spend restricts what you can stake, thus diminishing all future token income, which leads to even less voting power in the future.

Members who hold a disproportionate share of tokens can afford to out-spend on any vote's outcome and still retain proportional future voting power.

At best, you end up with powerful voting blocs, and at worst, a functional monopoly.

The internal discourse of Yield is, like all crypto, centered on the price of the DAO's scrip, not its actual functionality within the organization.

Rather than fostering a more equitable, democratic organization that caters to the needs of all its members, Yield is a scheme that explicitly rewards its highest stakeholders with increased power and access.

Now, theoretically, you could establish a DAO that works toward genuinely useful, worker-focused objectives, but you could also accomplish that without a DAO because it's merely an organization.

The DAO itself is simply a mechanism of an organization, and more often than not, its involvement is nothing more than tech fetishism.

So most actual DAOs do not resemble anything like a flat hierarchy.

In fact, the capacity to buy and sell voting power, along with the hierarchy that results, is perceived as a distinct advantage, as it allows emotionally detached members to profit and provides them with something they can use to reward individuals that will "align incentives," and despite the fact that Li Jin is directly associated with Yield as the "philosopher in residence," Yield is neither structured like a labor union nor does it aspire to be one.

The point is that thought leaders like Li Jin, who gain social traction by asserting that their technofetishistic community is solving significant societal issues, are deceivers.

They revel in the pageantry of democracy because it enables them to appear democratic and allows them to paint their critics as undemocratic.

It's all empty gestures and jargon to distract from the reality that it's just shareholding.

Chapter 25: The Corporatization of Everything

It's the corporatization of everything—the transformation of the entire world into enclaves governed by power granted through token possession and enforced by machines that permit humans to absolve themselves of the consequences.

At the end of the day, every DAO pretending to be useful is still a forced entry point into some hype-driven memecoin whose existence solely benefits its creators and the exchange that sells it.

In 2008, the economy essentially collapsed.

The basic chain reaction was this: bankers took mortgages and converted them into something they could gamble on.

This created a bubble, and then the bubble burst.

When you examine it closely, you realize that the core of the crypto ecosystem, the essence of Web3, and the foundation of the NFT marketplace is a turf battle between the affluent and ultra-affluent.

Technofetishists who look at figures like Bill Gates and Jeff Bezos—billionaires who emerged through tech industry avenues that have now been closed off by market stagnation—are seeking a second chance, hoping to forge a new market where they can ascend from merely wealthy programmers to hyper-wealthy industrialists.

It's a clawing contest between the top 5% and the top 1%.

Ultimately, the underlying forces driving this entire movement are economic inequality.

The wealthy and those precariously wealthy are searching for a space they can dominate, where they can be trendsetters and tastemakers, seemingly creating value through sheer will.

Conclusion: Deteriorating System

This is, in my view, the blind spot of many casual critics.

The fact that tokens representing ape profile pictures are worthless, yet still somehow command high prices, isn't a flaw in the system that's been overlooked; it's part of the design.

It's a digital extension of inconvenient fashion. It's a display of status and a form of myth-making.

And that's how it captivates the masses: individuals who perceive their opportunities dwindling, who see the system tightening around them, who have become isolated by social media and a global pandemic, who feel the future contracting, people pressured by the casualization of labor as jobs dissolve into the gig economy, and long to believe that escape is just that simple.

All you have to do is gamble on the right Discord, and you might be air-dropped the next big thing.

It could be you, selected from the crowd on Rarible and granted a six-figure price tag by an elusive Emirati music producer.

Acquire a BAYC for your wallet, hold it like a good diamond hand, and reap the rewards.

All you need is $5000 in initial capital to purchase a Farmer's World milk cow, and if you milk that cow every four hours, day and night, for two weeks, well, there's your investment back right there, and now it's all profit (minus, of course, the overhead costs for all the WAX you needed to stake, the barn you had to buy and construct, the barley you needed to buy and cultivate, the food required to replenish the energy needed to milk the cow, build the barn, and grow the barley, plus you actually need to cash out, which isn't being compensated, it's quitting).

This is your opportunity to take a stand against Wall Street and Venture Capitalists, as long as you ignore the VCs lurking behind the scenes.

The trajectory can only go upward.

It's a movement propelled in no small part by anger—by individuals who looked at 2008, who examined the existing system, yet concluded that the issues with capitalism were that it didn't provide enough chances to be the oppressor.

And that's the pitch. Buy in now, invest early, and you could become the high-tech future oppressor.

Our systems are either collapsing or already broken, straining under neglect and sabotage, while our leaders appear, at best, complacent, willing to coast through the collapse.

We need something better.

However, a system that transforms everyone into minor digital landlords, that reduces all interaction to transactions, that determines value based on how marketable something is and whether or not it can be gambled on as fractional tokens sold through micro-auctions — that's not the answer.

A different system doesn't inherently imply a superior system; we frequently replace poor systems with worse ones.

We swapped out a flawed work and management system for a dreadful framework of apps, gigs, and on-demand labor.

Thus, it's not merely that I oppose NFTs because the majority of them are aesthetically void representations of the hollow inner lives of the tech and finance enthusiasts behind them; it's that they signify the forefront of a deteriorating system.

The entirety of it—from OpenSea fantasies for starving artists to the buy-in for Play-to-Earn games—represents the same empty, exploitative pitch as multi-level marketing schemes. It's Amway, but everywhere you look, people are adorned with unattractive ape graphics.

www.ingramcontent.com/pod-product-compliance
Lightning Source LLC
Chambersburg PA
CBHW071024240526
45469CB00006BD/2070